GRAPHIS BROCHURES 2

After 11 years in Minneapolis, Duffy Design is proud to announce the opening of a New York office. Same dedication to brand development. Same relentless pursuit toward the best possible solution. Just a whole different view out the window.
DUFFY
NEW YORK, NEW YORK
212
DESIGN
duffy
brand id
corporate id
packaging

GRAPHIS BROCHURES 2

. . . .

AN INTERNATIONAL COMPILATION OF BROCHURE DESIGN

BROSCHÜRENDESIGN IM INTERNATIONALEN ÜBERBLICK

UNE COMPILATION INTERNATIONALE SUR LE DESIGN DES BROCHURES

EDITED BY • HERAUSGEGEBEN VON • EDITÉ PAR:

B. MARTIN PEDERSEN

PUBLISHER AND CREATIVE DIRECTOR: B. MARTIN PEDERSEN

BOOK PUBLISHER: CHRISTOPHER T. REGGIO

EDITORS: CLARE HAYDEN, HEINKE JENSSEN

ASSOCIATE EDITOR: PEGGY CHAPMAN

ART DIRECTOR: VALERIE MYERS

PRODUCTION ASSISTANT: CONSTANTINE FRANGOS

PHOTOGRAPHER: ALFREDO PARRAGA

GRAPHIS INC.

OPPOSITE: DUFFY DESIGN (IN-HOUSE)

CONTENTS

INHALT

SOMMAIRE

REMARKS

ANMERKUNGEN

ANNOTATIONS

WE EXTEND OUR HEARTFELT THANKS TO CONTRIBUTORS THROUGHOUT THE WORLD WHO HAVE MADE IT POSSIBLE TO PUBLISH A WIDE AND INTERNATIONAL SPECTRUM OF THE BEST WORK IN THIS FIELD.

ENTRY INSTRUCTIONS FOR ALL GRAPHIS BOOKS MAY BE REQUESTED FROM:
GRAPHIS INC.
141 LEXINGTON AVENUE
NEW YORK, NY 10016-8193

UNSER DANK GILT DEN EINSENDERN AUS ALLER WELT, DIE ES UNS DURCH IHRE BEITRÄGE ERMÖGLICHT HABEN, EIN BREITES, INTERNATIONALES SPEKTRUM DER BESTEN ARBEITEN ZU VERÖFFENTLICHEN.

TEILNAHMEBEDINGUNGEN FÜR DIE GRAPHIS-BÜCHER SIND ERHÄLTLICH BEIM:
GRAPHIS INC.
141 LEXINGTON AVENUE
NEW YORK, NY 10016-8193Z

TOUTE NOTRE RECONNAISSANCE VA AUX DESIGNERS DU MONDE ENTIER DONT LES ENVOIS NOUS ONT PERMIS DE CONSTITUER UN VASTE PANORAMA INTERNATIONAL DES MEILLEURES CRÉATIONS.

LES MODALITÉS D'INSCRIPTION PEUVENT ÊTRE OBTENUES AUPRÈS DE:
GRAPHIS INC.
141 LEXINGTON AVENUE
NEW YORK, NY 10016-8193

OPPOSITE: GOODBY SILVERSTEIN & PARTNERS/BELL HELMETS • FOLLOWING PAGE: LARSON DESIGN (IN -HOUSE)
THE ART DIRECTOR AND DESIGNER OF THE COVER PHOTOGRAPH FOR BROCHURES 1 AND BROCHURES 2 IS WERNER WÜRDINGER. THE PHOTOGRAPHER IS UWE ZISS. WE REGRET THEY WERE NOT CREDITED IN BROCHURES 1.

COMMENTARIES

KOMMENTARE

COMMENTAIRES

Pier Paolo Pitacco

As an art director and designer, I keep especially beautiful brochures I have designed in order to show them to clients. While the clients are satisfied with a brochure if it presents a new collection or product in the best possible way, for the consumer (whether a design expert or not) the brochure is above all an instrument of information which is often quickly forgotten immediately after it is used. In today's consumer society, things are quickly thrown away; we have all become novelty junkies, seemingly without time to stop and enjoy the small, beautiful things. • Brochures packed with images and advertising messages usually last just a few months. Therefore, I always try to design brochures with great emotional impact, so that one becomes curious and wants to possess them, just as one would want to possess a jacket, a piece of furniture, or other items which appeal to our aesthetic sense. Many consumeristic icons of this century such as the Rolex Daytona, Ferrari, or the clothes designed by great fashion designers are in high demand not just because they are status symbols, but also because of their high aesthetic appeal. This is

Pier Paolo Pitacco is a creative director at the Cento per Cento Graphic Design Studio in Milan, Italy. His many clients include Dolce & Gabbana, Byblos, and Swatch. He has won awards for his work from the Art Directors Club and has been widely published. Since 1977 he has been in charge of artistic production for L'Uomo Vogue and is currently art director for Elle Italia.

(PREVIOUS SPREAD, OPENING IMAGE) SHIRT PACKAGING FOR FALLBROOK. • (THIS PAGE, TOP LEFT IMAGE) TIE STAND DESIGNED AS PART OF AN IDENTITY CREATED FOR ITALSETA. (TOP ROW, RIGHT IMAGE) LIMITED EDITION BOOK SPONSORED BY THE PINO GIARDINI COMPANY. (BOTTOM ROW, LEFT AND CENTER IMAGES) SAMPLES OF COVER EDITORIAL DESIGN FOR YOU MAGAZINE. (BOTTOM RIGHT IMAGE) BROCHURE DESIGN FOR MISSONI KNITWEAR. • (OPPOSITE PAGE) PORTRAIT OF PIER PAOLO PITACCO BY ARMIN LINKE.

exactly the quality found in good brochure design. The goal is to design a brochure that makes one want to look at it, touch it, open it, and keep it. • To produce a brochure which both makes the product memorable and is of intrinsic aesthetic value to the consumer, one must avoid any superficial effects. The designer must be a master of the craft and make efficient use of all his or her tools. Although new digital techniques may help, what really matters is the sensibility with which the designer handles the different media and cultures. It does not suffice to deliver a product which is only highly efficient; it must also be unique and inspired. It is a real challenge to choose an unusual format or to break the "rules" and use fabric instead of paper, for example, or to use minimalistic typography which seamlessly transcends the text/image dichotomy, or very sensitive colors (such as the colors of the frescoes of Pompeii). Of course, there must be no superfluous elements; everything must be harmonious. • Brochures are more conducive to creativity and originality in design than are other media. They do not usually have as high a print run as a magazine, and therefore allow for experimentation. Generally, clients are prepared to pay a little more to have their products presented in a brochure, as they are aware their money will not buy them much advertising space in other print media. Brochures continue to be an attractive advertising medium which speaks directly to the heart of the consumer. The wide range of aesthetically pleasing designs found in this volume attests to the impact and staying power of a well-designed brochure.

Ich als Art Direktor und Designer hebe besonders schöne Broschüren, die wir gestaltet haben, auf, um sie Kunden zu zeigen oder bei Wettbewerben, wie z.B. dem Graphis-Brochures-Wettbewerb, einzusenden. ■ Dem Kunden genügt es, wenn seine neue Kollektion oder sein neues Produkt in seiner Broschüre zur Geltung kommt, aber natürlich soll das auf die bestmögliche Art geschehen. ■ Für den Endverbraucher, ob er nun Fachmann ist oder

PIER PAOLO PITACCO IST CREATIVE DIRECTOR VON CENTO PER CENTO, EINEM GRAPHIK-DESIGN-STUDIO IN MAILAND. SEINE ARBEITEN WURDEN MEHRFACH VOM ITALIENISCHEN ART DIRECTORS CLUB AUSGEZEICHNET UND IN VERSCHIEDENEN FACHPUBLIKATIONEN VORGESTELLT. SEIT 1977 IST ER FÜR DIE KÜNSTLERISCHE PRODUKTION DES MAGAZINS *L'UOMO VOGUE* VERANTWORTLICH. ZUR ZEIT IST ER ZUDEM ART DIRECTOR VON *ELLE ITALIA*.

nicht, ist die Broschüre in erster Linie ein reines Informationsmittel, das nach Gebrauch sofort in Vergessenheit gerät. Unsere heutige Gesellschaft neigt dazu, schnell wegzuwerfen, zu vergessen; wir sind alle so sehr zu Informations-Junkies geworden, dass scheinbar keine Zeit zum Innehalten bleibt, dass die Freude an schönen, kleinen Dingen verlorengeht. ■ Broschüren mit ihren vielen Bildern, Werbebotschaften und Informationen haben für gewöhnlich nur eine Lebensdauer von wenigen Monaten. Ich habe mich deshalb immer bemüht, Broschüren zu gestalten, die eine so grosse emotionale Wirkung haben, dass die Leute neugierig werden und sie schliesslich wie ein Objekt besitzen möchten, wie man eine Jacke oder ein Möbelstück oder andere Dinge besitzen möchte, die an unser ästhetisches Gefühl, an unsere Sehnsucht nach Schönheit appellieren. ■ Viele Konsum-Ikone unseres Jahrhunderts werden begehrt, weil sie Status-Symbole sind, aber auch weil sie ganz einfach schön sind. Ich denke dabei an die Rolex Daytona, an einen Ferrari oder auch an Kleider der grossen Mode-Designer. Genau das muss man mit einer Broschüre erreichen, man muss etwas entwerfen, das die Leute so sehr anspricht, dass sie es anfassen, öffnen, anschauen und schliesslich aufbewahren möchten. Damit bleibt auch das in der Broschüre vorgestellte Produkt unvergesslich. ■ Wenn das gelingt, haben wir das Maximum erreicht, indem aus dem Objekt, das so leicht vernachlässigt, vergessen und weggeworfen wird, ein begehrtes Objekt wird. Um das zu erreichen, muss der Gestalter auf oberflächliche Effekte

verzichten, und er muss all sein Können einsetzen und seine Werkzeuge beherrschen. Die Zukunft gehört nicht nur den neuen digitalen Möglichkeiten, es wird schliesslich immer nur auf den sensiblen Umgang mit den Medien und den Kulturen ankommen, und dazu gehören auch die traditionellen Techniken der alten Meister der bildenden Kunst: die Schlichtheit der Gesten, die Schönheit des Strichs. ■ Es genügt nicht, ein Produkt abzuliefern, das aus professioneller Sicht einwandfrei ist, sondern es muss phantasievoll und einzigartig sein. ■ Dabei ist es äusserst interessant, die Regeln auf den Kopf zu stellen, zum Beispiel, einfach Stoff statt Papier zu wählen, oder ein Format, das absolut ungewöhnlich ist, minimalistische Typographie, die mit dem Bild verschmilzt, oder sehr gefühlvolle Farben (für mich sind das die Farben der Fresken von Pompeji). Nichts darf überflüssig, alles muss harmonisch und wohlbegründet sein. Die Broschüre ist ein ideales Medium, um etwas Ungewöhnliches zu wagen. Sie hat allgemein keine so grosse Auflage wie z.B. Magazine, und damit lässt sie mehr Spielraum für Experimente. ■ Die Kunden sind durchaus bereit, etwas mehr dafür auszugeben, um ihre Produkte in Broschüren vorstellen zu können, zumal sie sich durchaus bewusst sind, dass ihr Geld nicht sehr weit reichen würde, wenn sie stattdessen Anzeigen schalten würden. Sie wissen sehr wohl, dass sie mit einer Broschüre ein attraktives Werbemittel in der Hand haben. Das erklärt auch, warum die Produktion eines so traditionellen Mediums wie die Broschüre und die entsprechende Nachfrage nach wie vor hoch sind.

Pour nous autres, directeurs artistiques et designers, une belle brochure se conserve avec le plus grand soin, car un jour où l'autre, elle forcera sans doute l'admiration d'un client ou s'attirera les faveurs d'une maison d'édition comme Graphis qui lui ouvrira les portes d'un concours. ▲ Pour le client, une brochure est avant tout un moyen de promouvoir sa dernière création maison. Certes, il n'a rien contre le fait qu'elle soit présentée sous son meilleur jour. Bien au contraire. ▲ Pour le consommateur, qu'il soit un spécialiste ou non, la brochure a un but purement informatif et, une fois consultée, elle perdra tout son attrait et sera vite jetée aux oubliettes. ▲ Dans notre société surmédiatisée, tout se consomme et se consume très vite, tout s'oublie. Jour après jour, nous avalons une quantité incroyable d'informations sans jamais prendre le temps de les digérer. Nous n'avons plus le temps de nous souvenir, de nous réjouir, d'apprécier les petites choses de la vie. ▲ En règle générale, les brochures, condensés d'images, de messages publicitaires et d'informations, ont une durée de vie de quelques mois. C'est pourquoi j'ai toujours mis un point d'honneur à leur donner un impact émotionnel tel qu'elles piquent la curiosité des consommateurs, fassent briller leurs yeux de convoitise et qu'une fois sous le charme, ces derniers n'aient plus qu'une envie, la posséder, comme l'on possède un meuble design, un tableau ou tout autre objet qui fait appel à notre sens de l'esthétique, à notre quête perpétuelle de beauté. ▲ Maintes icônes de notre société de consommation vivent du statut qu'elles confèrent à leur possesseur, mais aussi tout simplement parce qu'elles sont belles. Je pense, par exemple, à la Rolex Daytona, à une Ferrari ou encore aux sublimes créations des grands couturiers. Et pour une brochure, il ne devrait pas en être autrement. Il faut créer quelque chose que les gens aient envie de toucher, de caresser, comme une sculpture, quelque chose qu'ils

aient envie d'ouvrir, de regarder, comme un livre précieux. Quelque chose qu'ils aient envie de conserver. ▲ Si nous atteignons cet objectif, alors nous aurons fait le maximum, car l'objet autrefois négligé, oublié, voire jeté, sera désiré, convoité, jalousement gardé pour sa valeur esthétique et, de plus, il rappellera le produit pour lequel il a été créé. ▲ Le futur n'appartient pas exclusivement à l'ordinateur, ni aux possibilités infinies offertes par les programmes existants. Il s'agit bien plus de faire preuve de sensibilité, de fondre avec talent divers médias et cultures, de savoir utiliser à bon escient les techniques les plus diverses parmi lesquelles figurent également les techniques traditionnelles des grands maîtres de l'art pictural, qui honorent la simplicité du geste, la beauté du trait. ▲ Livrer un produit irréprochable aux yeux d'un professionnel ne suffit plus. Ce qu'il faut bien plus, c'est que le produit soit unique en son genre, qu'il transcende le temps, repousse les limites du connu. Dans ce contexte, il est intéressant de renverser la nature des choses, par exemple en remplaçant le papier par du tissu, en choisissant un format inhabituel, une typographie minimaliste qui se fond dans l'image, ou des couleurs chargées d'émotions (comme celles des mosaïques et peintures murales de Pompéi). ▲ Naturellement, rien ne doit être gratuit. Tout doit être rigueur et harmonie. Le tirage d'une brochure étant inférieur à celui d'un magazine, celle-ci représente un médium idéal pour tenter de nouvelles expériences. De plus, les clients sont tout à fait disposés à dépenser un peu plus pour présenter leur produit dans une brochure originale, sachant bien que le même argent ne suffirait pas à couvrir les espaces publicitaires autrement requis. Et ils savent également qu'une brochure est un excellent support publicitaire. Ne nous étonnons pas donc pas si la production d'un médium aussi traditionnel que la brochure ne fait pas que se perpétuer, mais augmente de façon constante.

PIER PAOLO PITACCO EST DIRECTEUR DE LA CRÉATION DE CENTO PER CENTO, UNE AGENCE DE DESIGN GRAPHIQUE À MILAN. SES TRAVAUX ONT ÉTÉ PRIMÉS À PLUSIEURS REPRISES PAR LE ART DIRECTORS CLUB ET PUBLIÉS DANS DE NOMBREUX OUVRAGES ET MAGAZINES SPÉCIALISÉS. DEPUIS 1977, IL EST RESPONSABLE DE LA PRODUCTION ARTISTIQUE DE L'UOMO VOGUE ET OCCUPE ACTUELLEMENT LE POSTE DE DIRECTEUR ARTISTIQUE D'ELLE ITALIA.

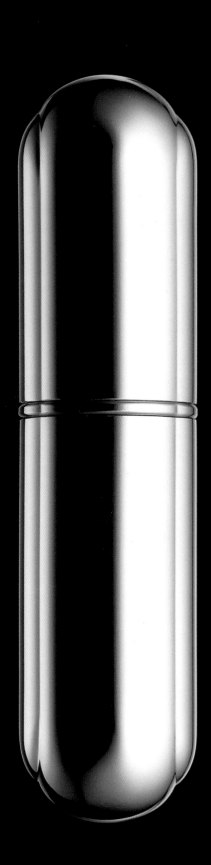

Taku Satoh

While I was a student in art school, teachers and others often told me how important it is for a creator to find his or her own style. I believe "style" in this sense refers to an approach with such originality that the audience immediately knows who created the work. After six years of college and graduate school searching in vain for a personal style, I became employed as a designer in a major advertising agency. I also continued to create works in my private time, intending to arm myself with my own style. As a result of attempting many different things, I realized I could not restrict myself to just one approach. I became reconciled to this fact, though I admit to a lingering attachment to the notion of a "visible style" that would be immediately recognized by all as my own. ■ I had never intended to work in advertising for life, and after three years I quit the company to become a freelance designer. The first job I took on encompassed the product development of a whiskey, as well as its packaging and communication strategy. Because this work progressed independently, I was able to reflect on all of my concerns: what

TAKU SATOH IS THE FOUNDER OF TAKU SATOH DESIGN IN TOKYO, JAPAN. THE RECIPIENT OF NUMEROUS DESIGN AND ADVERTISING AWARDS, SATOH EARNED HIS MASTERS IN DESIGN FROM TOKYO NATIONAL UNIVERSITY OF FINE ARTS AND MUSIC. ONE OF HIS MANY MAJOR CLIENTS INCLUDES MAX FACTOR. IN ADDITION TO HIS FULL-TIME DESIGN WORK, SATOH IS A PERCUSSIONIST AND PLAYS MERENGUE MUSIC WITH "ALASKA BAND."

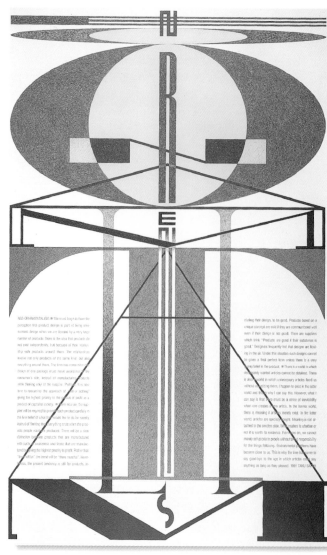

I thought the problem points with whiskey were, my awareness of the questions related to product development itself, and my doubts about advertising methods of the day. ● This first job was a success and later earned me design and product development work. I became involved with many design genres, including cosmetics design, packaging design for food products, and the design of tools such as rulers. After several years I wondered what my style had become. By then I had completely lost the awareness of being a creator which I had as a student, and possessed a strong consciousness of myself as a designer. ● The brochure entitled "Neo-Ornamentalism" was from a private exhibition of mine which I developed both to show others my designs and to somehow verify those designs for myself. This brochure was meant to show the product design as simply as possible, and accordingly, only one product was featured per page. The exhibition and brochure were the results of considering the parameters of the project, finding the appropriate methods, and making the effort to realize my ideas. After the exhibition I understood there were no recurring visual themes running through my work, but I then began to think of it as having its own "invisible style." There was no common method in the work I did following the exhibition either, not even in mass product design and poster graphic design. In my poster design, for example, I used a variety of methods and materials including pencil, photography, even a "crushed" product I previously designed. I used whatever I felt to be the most appropriate method for a given project. ● My next brochure will be for a private exhibition of a modern artist, but will be very different from the typical exhibition brochure, and I plan to make the text central. No matter how small the project, I always try to approach it with an open and objective mind. I'm not even able to clearly define "invisible style", but I believe the only way to proceed is to do a lot of work without focusing on the question of style. Unless I'm a big fan, I don't want to see the face of the designer in the goods that surround us in our daily lives. I've recently come to believe that this is a valid stance for a designer. Previously people around me would say I should put more individuality into my work, but strangely enough I haven't heard this recently.

Als ich noch die Kunstschule besuchte, bekam ich von den Lehrern und anderen Leuten immer wieder zu hören, wie wichtig es für einen Gestalter sei, seinen eigenen Stil zu finden. Ich glaube, dass dabei mit «Stil» die persönliche Auffassung gemeint war, die soviel Originalität haben musste, dass der Urheber einer Arbeit für das Publikum leicht erkennbar war. Nach sechs Jahren im College, in denen ich mich vergeblich um einen persönlichen Stil bemüht hatte, fand ich eine Stelle als Graphiker in einer grossen Werbeagentur. Ich arbeitete auch in meiner Freizeit, in der Absicht, zu einem eigenen Stil zu gelangen. Nachdem ich verschiedene Dinge ausprobiert hatte, wurde mir klar, dass ich nicht mehr wie bisher nur eine Sache tun durfte, und dass an diesem Zug meines Charakters nichts zu ändern war. Das versöhnte mich, obgleich ich zugeben muss, dass die Vorstellung eines «persönlichen Stils», den man sofort als den meinen erkennen würde, mich nach wie vor reizte. ■ Ich hatte nie vorgehabt, für die Werbung zu arbeiten, und nach drei Jahren verliess ich die Firma, um als freier Graphiker zu arbeiten. Mein erster Auftrag erstreckte sich auf die Produktentwicklung eines Whiskys, wozu auch die Packungsgestaltung und die Kommunikationsstrategie gehörten. Ich hatte dabei Gelegenheit, darüber nachzudenken, was nach meiner Meinung die Problempunkte des Whiskys waren, welche Fragen sich für mich im Zusammenhang mit der Herstellung des Produktes stellen würden und was mich an den derzeit üblichen Werbemethoden störte. Dieser erste Auftrag hat mir persönlich viel gebracht und auch danach zu Design- und Produktentwicklungsaufträgen verholfen. Ich hatte mit vielen Bereichen des Designs zu tun, u.a. mit Kosmetikprodukten, Verpackungen für Nahrungsmittel und mit der Gestaltung von graphischen Werkzeugen wie zum Beispiel Lineale. Nach einigen Jahren fragte ich mich, ob ich wohl einen eigenen Stil entwickelt hatte. Ich hatte mittlerweile das in der Schule noch allgegenwärtige Bewusstsein, ein Künstler zu sein, völlig vergessen und betrachtete mich inzwischen als Designer. ■ Die Broschüre mit dem Titel «Neo-Ornamentalism» gehört zu einer privaten Ausstellung meiner Arbeiten. Hier war es darum gegangen, das Projekt zu analysieren, die geeigneten Methoden zu finden und die Ideen in die Tat umzusetzen. Um das Produkt-Design so einfach wie möglich zu präsentieren, wurde pro Seite nur ein Produkt gezeigt. Ich habe die Broschüre entworfen, um anden zu zeigen, was ich mache, aber auch für mich selbst, um mich damit

(PREVIOUS SPREAD, OPENING IMAGE) PACKAGING DESIGN FOR KANEBO ROUGE MAKEUP. ● (THIS SPREAD, OPPOSITE PAGE, TOP ROW) POSTERS FOR TAKU SATOH DESIGN OFFICE, INC. IN TOKYO, JAPAN. (BOTTOM ROW, LEFT IMAGE) PACKAGING DESIGN CREATED FOR LOTTE GREEN GUM. (BOTTOM ROW, RIGHT IMAGE) PACKAGING DESIGN CREATED FOR NITTOH SUPER-TEA BAG. ● (THIS PAGE) POSTER DESIGNED FOR BANG & OLUFSEN. ● (FOLLOWING PAGE) PORTRAIT OF TAKU SATOH BY TAMOTSU FUJII.

15

auseinanderzusetzen. Die Ausstellung bot mir Gelegenheit, all meine Arbeiten zusammen zu betrachten. Ich war überzeugt, einen bestimmten Stil entdecken zu müssen, aber nach der Ausstellung war mir klar, dass es einfach keine visuellen Themen gibt, die sich wie ein roter Faden durch meine Arbeit ziehen. Ich begann, an einen «unsichtbaren Stil» zu denken. ■ Auch bei den Arbeiten, die ich danach machte, gab es keine einheitliche Methode, nicht einmal bei Produkten für den Massenmarkt oder etwa bei den Plakaten. Für diese arbeitete ich zum Beispiel mit Bleistift oder mit Photographie oder sogar, wie kürzlich, mit einem 'zerdrückten' Produkt. Diese ganz unterschiedlichen Methoden erklären sich dadurch, dass ich bei jeder Arbeit zuerst einmal eine neutrale Position beziehe und dann die Methode wähle, die mir am geeignetsten erscheint, und selbst bei einer ganz kleinen

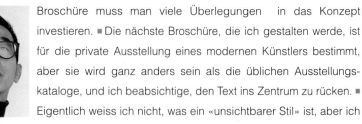

Broschüre muss man viele Überlegungen in das Konzept investieren. ■ Die nächste Broschüre, die ich gestalten werde, ist für die private Ausstellung eines modernen Künstlers bestimmt, aber sie wird ganz anders sein als die üblichen Ausstellungskataloge, und ich beabsichtige, den Text ins Zentrum zu rücken. ■ Eigentlich weiss ich nicht, was ein «unsichtbarer Stil» ist, aber ich glaube, die einzig mögliche Art des Vorgehens ist, jedes Projekt mit neuen Augen zu sehen. Ich für meinen Teil möchte in den Dingen, die uns in unserem Alltag umgeben, nicht die Handschrift eines bestimmten Designers wiedererkennen, es sei denn, ich verehre ihn sehr. Mittlerweile bin ich zu der Überzeugung gelangt, dass dies die richtige Einstellung für einen Designer ist. Die Leute haben übrigens inzwischen aufgehört zu sagen, dass meine Arbeiten einen persönlicheren Stil brauchen.

Lorsque j'étais encore étudiant à l'école des arts appliqués, les professeurs nous disaient souvent à quel point il est important pour un concepteur de trouver son propre style. Je suppose que par «style», on entend dans ce contexte une approche si originale que tout le monde reconnaît au premier coup d'œil la griffe de l'artiste. Après six années d'études supérieures durant lesquelles j'ai essayé – en vain – de trouver un style personnel, j'ai décroché un travail de designer graphique dans une grande agence de publicité. En privé, je continuais à travailler pour moi, toujours en quête de ce style qui marquerait de mon empreinte, reconnaissable entre mille, chacune de mes créations. A force d'expérimenter tout et rien, j'ai commencé à comprendre certaines choses. J'ai réalisé que je ne pouvais me focaliser sur une seule chose à la fois, et rien ne pouvait changer cet aspect de ma personnalité. J'ai accepté ce fait, même si j'étais toujours très attaché à cette idée de «style visible», lequel me démarquerait de tous les autres. Je n'ai jamais eu l'intention de travailler toute ma vie dans le monde de la publicité et, après trois années de loyaux services, j'ai quitté la société pour me mettre à mon compte. Le premier mandat que l'on m'a confié concernait une marque de whisky. Il s'agissait à la fois de développer le produit, son packaging et la stratégie de communication. Durant cette période, j'ai pu me concentrer sur les problèmes inhérents au whisky, les questions qui se poseraient à moi dans le cadre de la production du produit et ce qui me déplaisait dans les méthodes publicitaires de l'époque. Ce premier travail en tant qu'indépendant m'a beaucoup apporté et m'a permis par la suite de travailler dans les domaines du design et du développement de produits. Mes tâches allaient du design de cosmétiques au packaging de produits alimentaires, en passant par la conception d'outils de travail tels que des règles. Après plusieurs années, je me suis demandé ce que mon style était devenu. A cette époque, je ne pensais plus, comme durant mes années d'études, être un créateur, mais me considérais uniquement comme un designer. ▲ La brochure intitulée «Neo-Ornamentalism» provient d'une exposition privée que j'ai conçue afin de présenter mes travaux et de

pouvoir jeter un regard plus critique sur mes réalisations. Elle devait présenter le design de produits le plus simplement du monde et, pour cette raison, un seul produit figure sur chaque page. L'exposition et la brochure cristallisaient les résultats obtenus dans le cadre de ce projet pour lequel j'avais dû tenir compte de plusieurs paramètres, trouver les méthodes adéquates et m'efforcer au mieux de réaliser mes idées. J'avais pensé qu'un style unitaire se dégagerait de tous ces travaux étant donné que j'en étais l'unique auteur, mais, après l'exposition, j'ai compris qu'il n'y avait pas de thèmes visuels récurrents. C'est alors que l'idée d'un style invisible a commencé à germer dans mon esprit. ▲ Par la suite, mes travaux ne présentaient plus aucun dénominateur commun, ni pour le design de produits destinés à la consommation de masse ni pour le graphisme d'affiches. Pour celles-ci, j'ai utilisé diverses méthodes et matériaux, le crayon, la photographie, même un produit «écrasé» que j'avais conçu auparavant. L'application de toutes ces méthodes résultait de l'approche que j'avais face à tout nouveau projet; à chaque fois, je jetais un regard neuf, parfaitement neutre sur la situation et j'essayais de trouver les méthodes les plus percutantes. ▲ J'ai réalisé ma première brochure parce que je ressentais le besoin d'apprécier mon propre design. Chaque projet, même si ce n'est qu'une brochure personnelle, repose toujours sur un concept, se construit à partir d'une idée à géométrie variable. Ma prochaine brochure qui sera consacrée à l'exposition d'un artiste contemporain se démarquera des brochures généralement réalisées pour ce genre de manifestation; je pense faire du texte l'élément central. Dans le fond, je ne sais pas ce qu'est un «style invisible», mais je crois que la seule approche possible est de considérer chaque projet avec un regard neuf. Pour ma part, je n'aimerais pas reconnaître dans les objets qui nous entourent au quotidien la signature d'un designer précis, à moins que je ne lui voue une admiration illimitée. Voilà au point où j'en suis arrivé aujourd'hui. Entre-temps les gens ont cessé de dire que mes travaux devraient avoir un style plus personnel.

Taku Satoh ist Gründer von Taku Satoh Design in Tokio. Satoh erhielt den Masters-Titel in Design von der Tokyo National University of Fine Arts and Music. Für seine Arbeiten hat er zahlreiche nationale und internationale Auszeichnungen der Design- und Werbebranche erhalten. Satoh ist nicht nur Gestalter, sondern auch Schlagzeuger und Mitglied der Alaska Band.

Taku Satoh est fondateur de Taku Satoh Design à Tokyo. Titulaire d'une maîtrise en design de la Tokyo National University of Fine Arts and Music, Satoh a remporté de nombreux prix aussi bien pour ses travaux de designer que pour ses réalisations publicitaires. Satoh ne se contente pas d'être un concepteur hors pair, il est également batteur et joue avec le groupe «Alaska Band».

BROCHURE DESIGN

BROSCHÜRENGESTALTUNG

DESIGN DES BROCHURES

RBMM/THE RICHARDS GROUP *AZROCK INDUSTRIES*

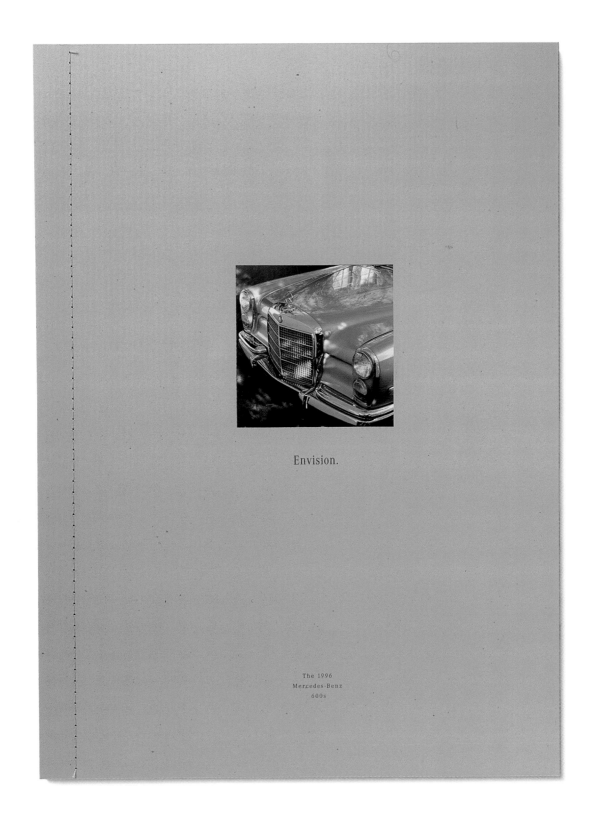

Envision.

The 1996
Mercedes-Benz
600s

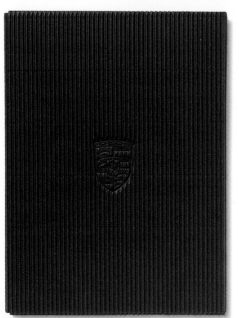

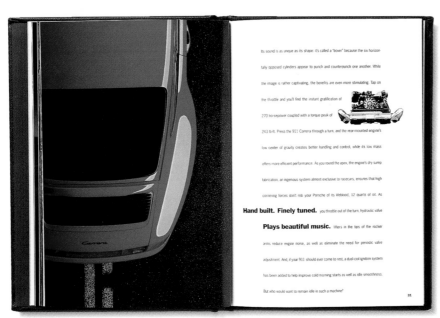

Its sound is as unique as its shape: it's called a "boxer" because the six horizontally opposed cylinders appear to punch and counterpunch one another. While the image is rather captivating, the benefits are even more stimulating. Tap on the throttle and you'll find the instant gratification of 270 horsepower coupled with a torque peak of 243 lb-ft. Press the 911 Carrera through a turn, and the rear-mounted engine's low center of gravity creates better handling and control, while its low mass offers more efficient performance. As you round the apex, the engine's dry sump lubrication, an ingenious system almost exclusive to racecars, ensures that high cornering forces don't rob your Porsche of its lifeblood, 12 quarts of oil. As **Hand built. Finely tuned.** you throttle out of the turn, hydraulic valve **Plays beautiful music.** lifters in the tips of the rocker arms, reduce engine noise, as well as eliminate the need for periodic valve adjustment. And, if your 911 should ever come to rest, a dual-coil ignition system has been added to help improve cold morning starts as well as idle smoothness. But who would want to remain idle in such a machine?

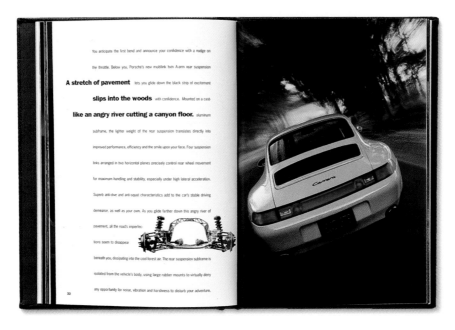

You anticipate the first bend and announce your confidence with a nudge on the throttle. Below you, Porsche's new multilink twin A-arm rear suspension **A stretch of pavement** lets you glide down the black strip of excitement **slips into the woods** with confidence. Mounted on a cast- **like an angry river cutting a canyon floor.** aluminum subframe, the lighter weight of the rear suspension translates directly into improved performance, efficiency and the smile upon your face. Four suspension links arranged in two horizontal planes precisely control rear wheel movement for maximum handling and stability, especially under high lateral acceleration. Superb anti-dive and anti-squat characteristics add to the car's stable driving demeanor, as well as your own. As you glide farther down this angry river of pavement, all the road's imperfec- tions seem to disappear beneath you, dissipating into the cool forest air. The rear suspension subframe is isolated from the vehicle's body, using large rubber mounts to virtually deny any opportunity for noise, vibration and harshness to disturb your adventure.

THE DESIGNORY, INC. *PORSCHE CARS NORTH AMERICA*

Dreams

Mercedes-Benz SL-Class

Inspiration

Mercedes-Benz C-Class

Desires

Mercedes-Benz S-Class

Imagine

Mercedes-Benz E-Class

The new 1996 Mercedes SL-Class.

THE DESIGNORY, INC. *Mercedes-Benz of North America, Inc.*

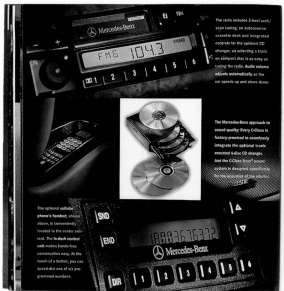

The radio includes 2-level seek/scan tuning, an autoreverse cassette deck and integrated controls for the optional CD changer, so selecting a track on compact disc is as easy as tuning the radio. Audio volume adjusts automatically as the car speeds up and slows down.

The Mercedes-Benz approach to sound quality: Every C-Class is factory-prewired to seamlessly integrate the optional trunk-mounted 6-disc CD changer. And the C-Class Bose® sound system is designed specifically for the acoustics of the interior.

The optional cellular phone's handset, shown above, is conveniently located in the center arm-rest. The in-dash control unit makes hands-free conversation easy. At the touch of a button, you can speed-dial one of six pro-grammed numbers.

Both C-Class audio systems use eight acoustically matched speakers to help create full, rich sound whether you're seated in front or rear. The speaker system that's standard on the C220 offers a high level of audio fidelity. A Bose® sound system created exclusively for the C-Class is standard on the C280 and optional on the C220. For lifelike music reproduction, reflex enclosures create bass response that's strong, tight and true. The optional cellular telephone, developed for the C-Class by Motorola, integrates seamlessly with the interior's design and function. Designed to be hands-free, it includes an in-dash control unit and a ceiling-mounted microphone to allow you to handle most calls without using the handset. Because the audio and cellular phone systems are integrated, the stereo automatically mutes whenever a call is received. And a separate cellular antenna isn't needed: it's incorporated within the power radio antenna.

For safety reasons, the driver should not use the actual telephone while the vehicle is in motion. We encourage the driver to stop the vehicle at a safe location before answering or placing a call.

What will it take to fulfill them?

Where will your desires drive you?

Chances are, you've driven luxury cars before. But none that evokes the pleasure you feel just by looking at the new E-Class. At a time when most other luxury sedans seem to have settled for design updates hardly distinguishable from their predecessors, the Mercedes-Benz E-Class moves decisively ahead. With a sensuous new shape that will likely remain fresh and engaging well into the next decade. And just think, the new E-Class manages to stir your emotions even before you do the most compelling thing of all: drive it.

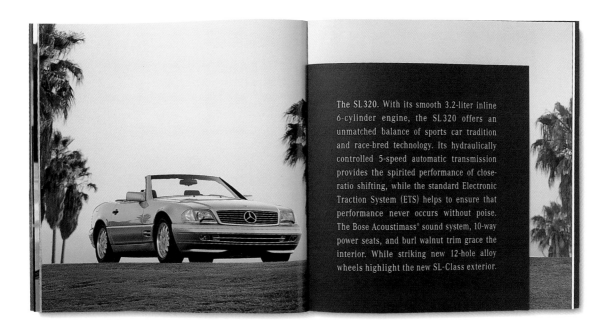

The SL320. With its smooth 3.2-liter inline 6-cylinder engine, the SL320 offers an unmatched balance of sports car tradition and race-bred technology. Its hydraulically controlled 5-speed automatic transmission provides the spirited performance of close-ratio shifting, while the standard Electronic Traction System (ETS) helps to ensure that performance never occurs without poise. The Bose Acoustimass® sound system, 10-way power seats, and burl walnut trim grace the interior. While striking new 12-hole alloy wheels highlight the new SL-Class exterior.

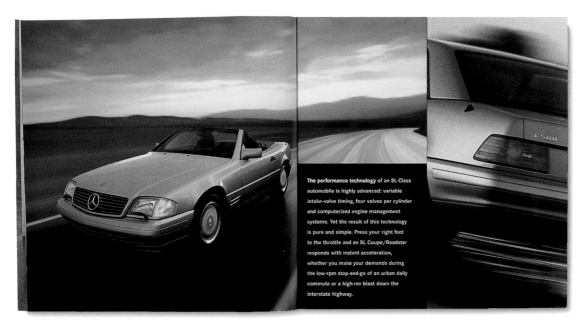

The performance technology of an SL-Class automobile is highly advanced: variable intake-valve timing, four valves per cylinder and computerized engine management systems. Yet the result of this technology is pure and simple. Press your right foot to the throttle and an SL Coupe/Roadster responds with instant acceleration, whether you make your demands during the low-rpm stop-and-go of an urban daily commute or a high-rev blast down the interstate highway.

When did the sky get so blue?

THE DESIGNORY, INC. *MERCEDES-BENZ OF NORTH AMERICA, INC.*

Sicher ist sicher
Ford zum Thema Sicherheit

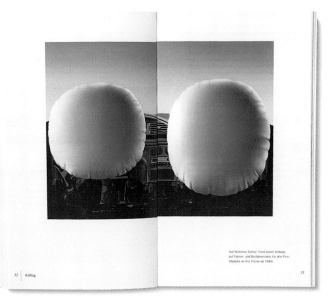

HANS GÜNTER SCHMITZ *Ford-Werke AG*

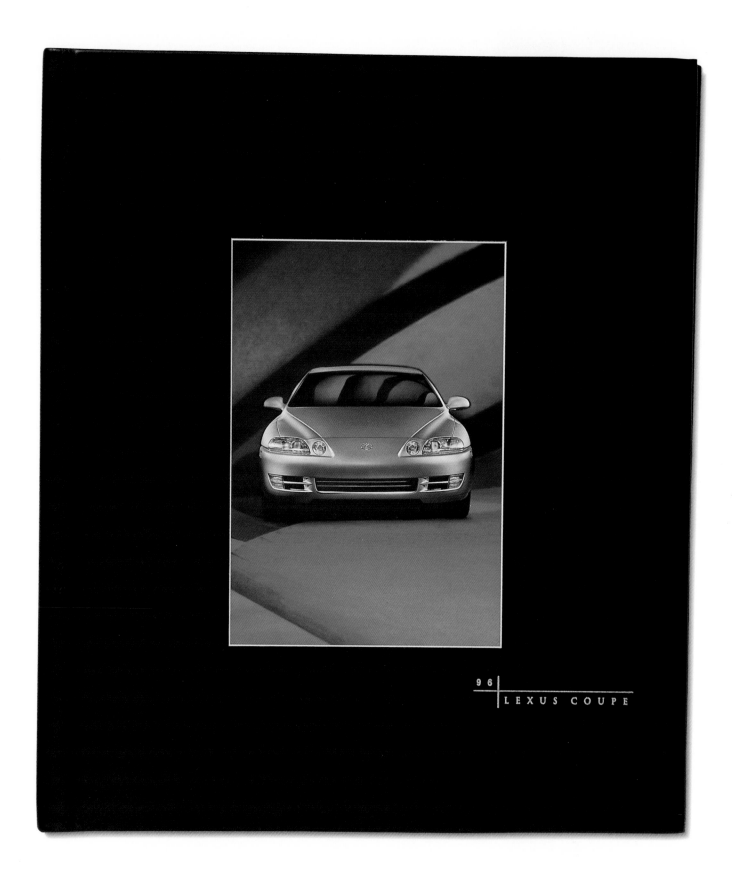

TEAM ONE ADVERTISING *Lexus*

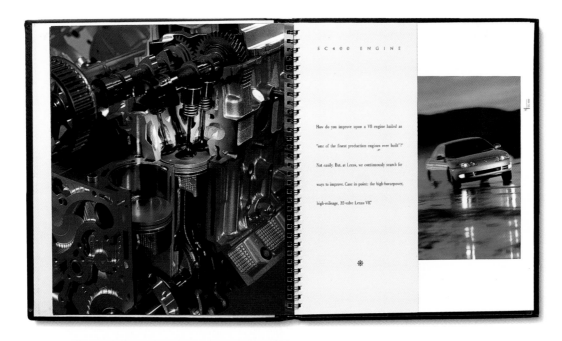

SC400 ENGINE

How do you improve upon a V8 engine hailed as
"one of the finest production engines ever built"?
Not easily. But, at Lexus, we continuously search for
ways to improve. Case in point: the high-horsepower,
high-mileage, 32-valve Lexus V8.

❋

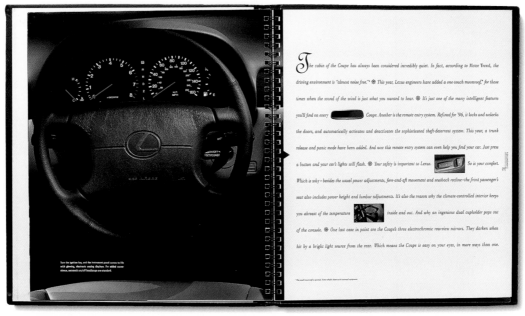

𝒯he cabin of the Coupe has always been considered incredibly quiet. In fact, according to Motor Trend, the driving environment is "almost noise free." ❋ This year, Lexus engineers have added a one-touch moonroof, for those times when the sound of the wind is just what you wanted to hear. ❋ It's just one of the many intelligent features you'll find on every ▬ Coupe. Another is the remote entry system. Refined for '96, it locks and unlocks the doors, and automatically activates and deactivates the sophisticated theft-deterrent system. This year, a trunk release and panic mode have been added. And now this remote entry system can even help you find your car. Just press a button and your car's lights will flash. ❋ Your safety is important to Lexus. So is your comfort. Which is why - besides the usual power adjustments, fore-and-aft movement and seatback recline - the front passenger's seat also includes power height and lumbar adjustments. It's also the reason why the climate-controlled interior keeps you abreast of the temperature inside and out. And why an ingenious dual cupholder pops out of the console. ❋ One last case in point are the Coupe's three electrochromic rearview mirrors. They darken when hit by a bright light source from the rear. Which means the Coupe is easy on your eyes, in more ways than one.

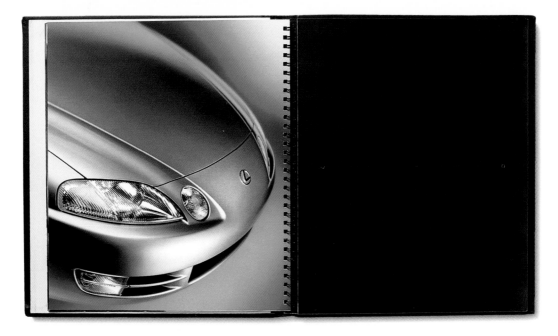

THE DESIGNORY, INC. *MITSUBISHI MOTOR SALES OF AMERICA, INC.*

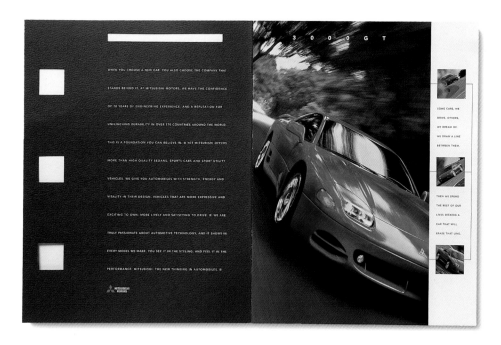

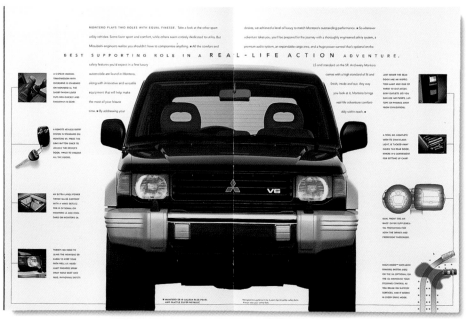

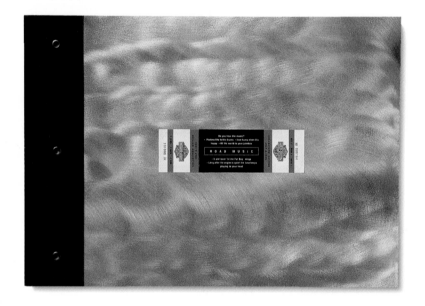

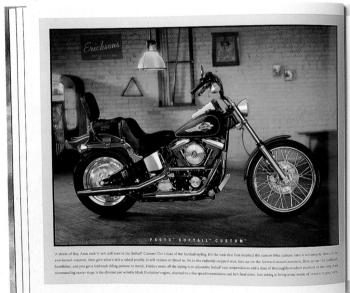

CARMICHAEL LYNCH *Harley-Davidson Motor Company*

ALL THE WORLD IS YOUR JUKEBOX.

Pick a road. An old highway headed out of town to nowhere. Six lanes of interstate rubbing shoulders with the cornfields. Neon-drenched strip or tree-lined lane. It doesn't matter where you're going or which connect like a song lyric when you travel on two. It's why we never stop refining the motorcycle itself. Like the sequential port fuel injection now available on many of our touring rigs. Or the new Riding a Harley® transforms the average stretch of pavement. You find the rhythm of the road. Gravel crunching under tires. A bumblebee joining up with your leathers. Things that pass without notice on stereo that's matched up with our timeless Electra Glide® fairing. Riders will even notice a new sound to the speakers. Although with a world like this, it may be awhile before the radio's turned on.

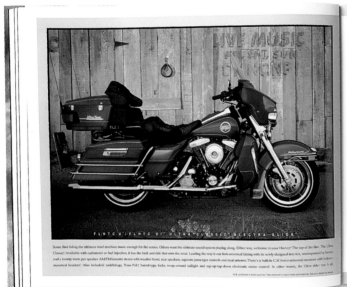

FLHTC U®/FLHTC UI® ULTRA CLASSIC® ELECTRA GLIDE®

Some find riding the ultimate road machine music enough for the senses. Others want the ultimate sound system playing along. Either way, welcome to your Harley.® The top of the line. The Ultra Classic.® Available with carburetor or fuel injection, it has the look and ride that own the road. Leading the way is our fork-mounted fairing with its newly-designed interior, accompanied by lowers and a twenty watts per speaker AM/FM/cassette stereo with weather band, rear speakers, separate passenger controls and dual antenna. There's a built-in C.B./voice-activated intercom with bolt-on mounted headset.® Also included: saddlebags, Tour-Pak,® barrel-type locks, wrap-around taillight and top-up-top-down electronic cruise control. In other words, the Ultra rider has it all.

FLTC UI® ULTRA CLASSIC® TOUR GLIDE®

How's this for majestic? The frame-mounted fairing adds out-and-out stature to the Ultra Classic® Tour Glide.® The features packed in behind make the ride feel every inch as good as it looks. Big, soft seat and passenger backrest. Twenty watts per speaker AM/FM/cassette stereo with weather band, rear speakers, remote passenger control and dual antenna. C.B./voice-activated intercom with bolt-on mounted headset.® Top-up-top-down electronic cruise control. Saddlebags and Tour-Pak® with interior lining and room for two full-face helmets. Barrel-type locks. Up on the handlebar you see the sleek new hand controls featured on all '96 models. Attached to the throttle is a fuel-injected Evolution® V-twin. Finished in chrome and black and ready to head for parts unknown.

IT AIN'T OVER 'TIL THE FAT BOY® SINGS.

Of all the places inspiration can take root and grow and become something awe-inspiring, there is no more fertile ground than the steel frame of a Harley-Davidson.® Just look at the line of motorcycles improving on the theme. To make it unmistakably your own, Harley-Davidson Genuine Motor Accessories® are the way to do it right. They're as steeped in our heritage and our tradition parked outside any place riders gather. You can't help but notice. Somewhere just beyond the pure, unadulterated joy that comes from owning a Harley.® The urge to start customizing takes hold the motorcycle itself. You put the same poetry into motion. Everything fits. Everything works. Like the old saying goes, they may laugh when you pick up the wrench. But then you start to play.

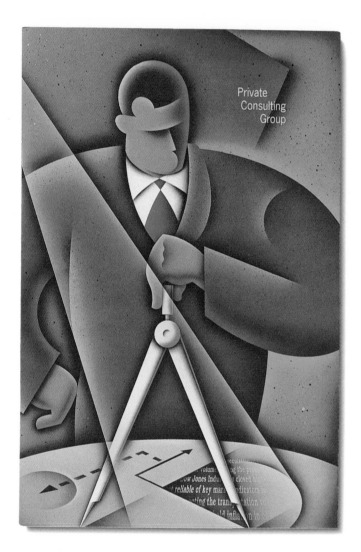

(Left) **CARLA HALL DESIGN GROUP** *CS First Boston*
(Right) **RHODES STAFFORD WINES CREATIVE** *Texas Instruments*

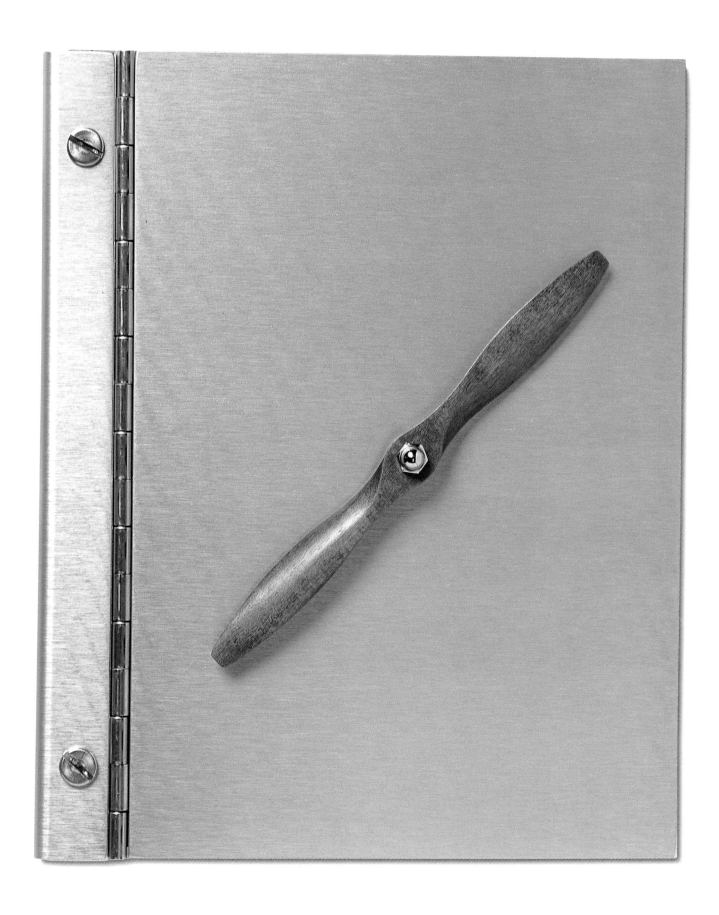

SLAUGHTER-HANSON *AMSOUTH BANK*

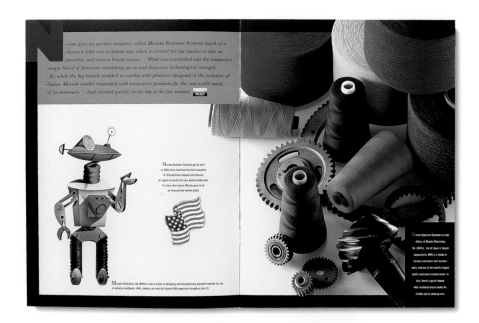

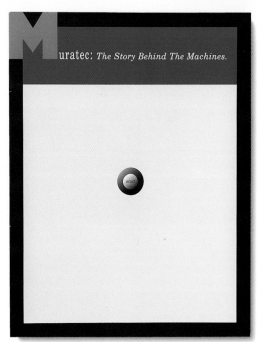

RBMM/THE RICHARDS GROUP *MURATA BUSINESS SYSTEMS*

THERE ARE 1,201,337* DOGS WITH THE NAME "BUDDY."

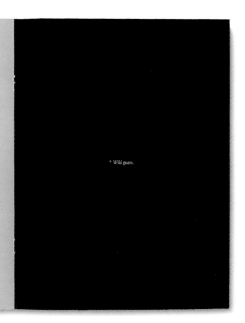

* Wild guess.

There are 79,416* men with the name Jim Smith.

* The Jim Smith Club of America.

There are 2,442* companies with the name "Northwestern" something-or-other.

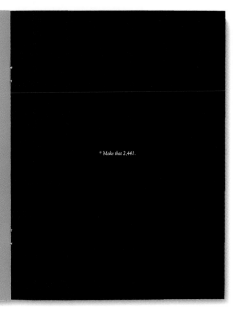

* Make that 2,441.

CLARITY COVERDALE FURY *RELIASTAR FINANCIAL*

NODDLE DEVELOPMENT COMPANY

BAILEY LAUERMAN & ASSOCIATES, INC. *NODDLE DEVELOPMENT COMPANY*

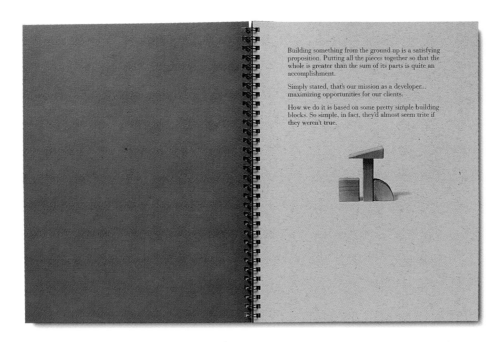

Building something from the ground up is a satisfying proposition. Putting all the pieces together so that the whole is greater than the sum of its parts is quite an accomplishment.

Simply stated, that's our mission as a developer... maximizing opportunities for our clients.

How we do it is based on some pretty simple building blocks. So simple, in fact, they'd almost seem trite if they weren't true.

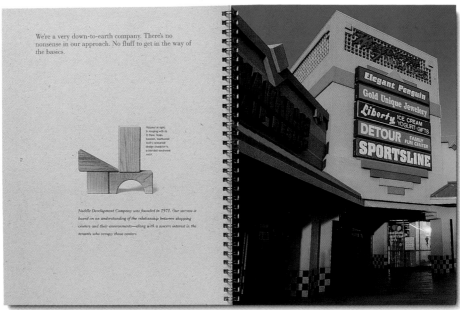

We're a very down-to-earth company. There's no nonsense in our approach. No fluff to get in the way of the basics.

Pictured at right, in keeping with its El Paso, Texas, location, Southwest Wolf's remodeled design character is a blended southwest motif.

Noddle Development Company was founded in 1971. Our success is based on an understanding of the relationship between shopping centers and their environments—along with a sincere interest in the tenants who occupy those centers.

But we wouldn't be growing as quickly or satisfying so many clients if we didn't possess two more equally important assets: a level of excitement for what we do and a sense of pride in quality that's unsurpassed.

Pictured at left, completed in 1983 in Lincoln, Nebraska, this is the first Super K-Mart in the western United States. Its 200,000 square foot Gateway, a full line discount store and supermarket.

To learn more about what we do and how we do it, call Noddle Development Company at 800-365-1616.

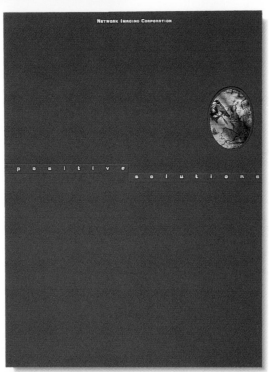

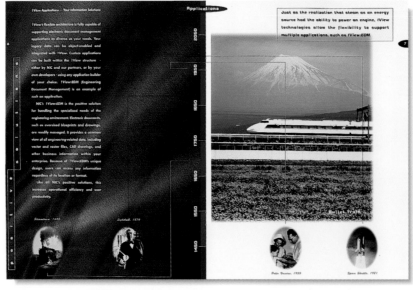

NETWORK IMAGING SYSTEMS CORPORATION *(IN-HOUSE)*

SAGMEISTER, INC. *SCHERTLER*

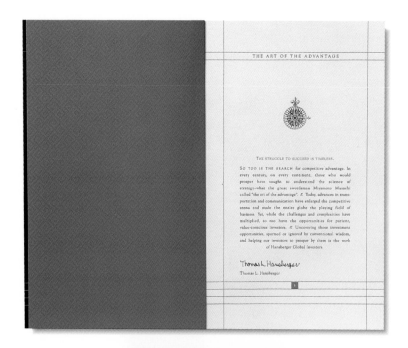

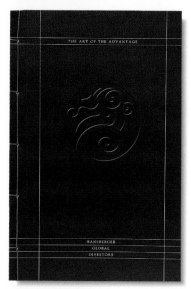

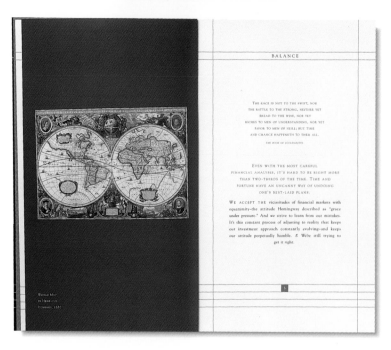

PENTAGRAM DESIGN *HANSBERGER GLOBAL INVESTORS*

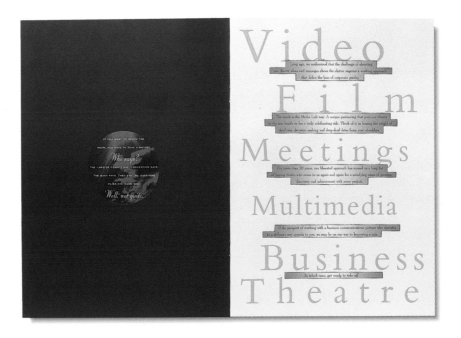

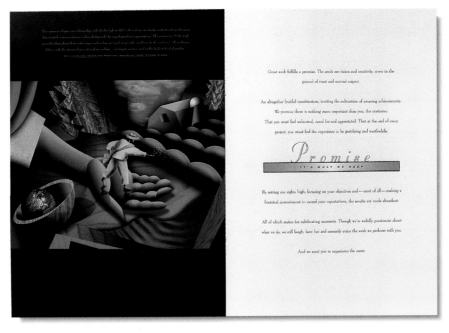

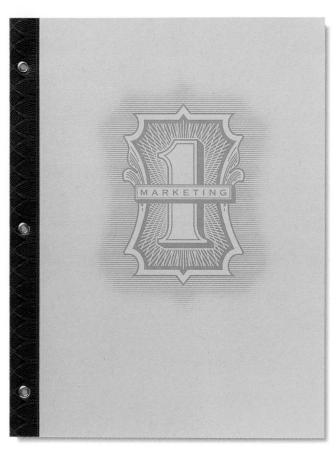

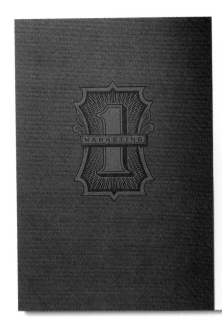

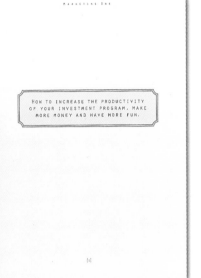

Marketing One

HOW TO INCREASE THE PRODUCTIVITY
OF YOUR INVESTMENT PROGRAM, MAKE
MORE MONEY AND HAVE MORE FUN.

[1]

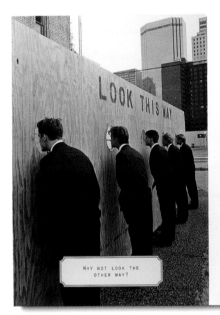

LOOK THIS WAY

WHY NOT LOOK THE
OTHER WAY?

Marketing One

IT'S AMAZING WHAT HAPPENS when an investment program becomes highly productive. Everybody gets taken care of and your program becomes more profitable. We have the best tools around to make that happen. Our ability to provide the right kinds of products and services comes from our ability to look at things from the proper perspective. One that incorporates steady growth far into the future.

We understand that you have the special responsibility of dealing with someone's life savings. We never forget that. If we can give you the right tools to help your customers and increase your program's productivity, then we're doing our job correctly.

To increase productivity, we must first look at what's causing poor performance. Low productivity can be attributed to many factors from a poor choice of products, to poor marketing, to a case of promoting transactions rather than relationships. Fortunately, we can turn around many situations. By offering a wide range of services along with our products, Marketing One can improve your program and build confidence throughout your customer base. And isn't that what you really want?

[?]

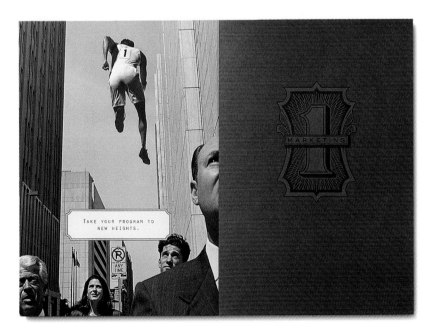

TAKE YOUR PROGRAM TO
NEW HEIGHTS.

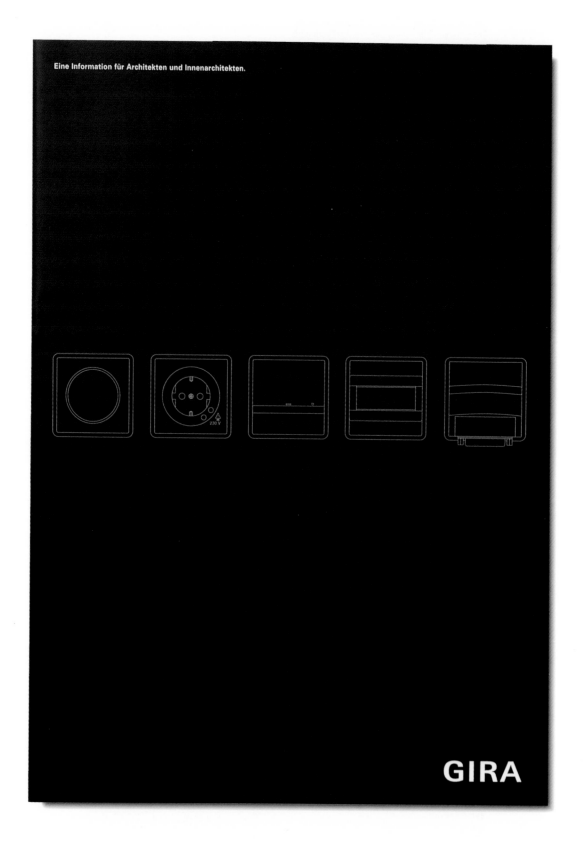

Eine Information für Architekten und Innenarchitekten.

GIRA

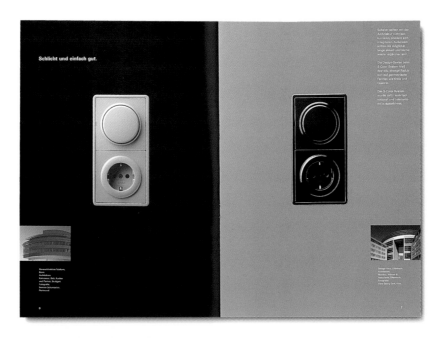

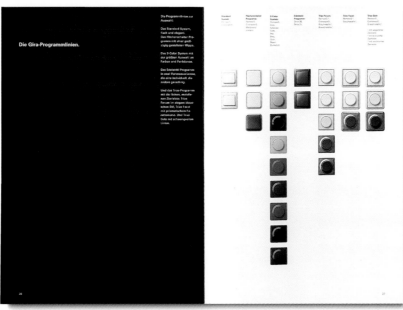

HANS GÜNTER SCHMITZ *GIRA, GIERSIEPEN GMBH & CO. KG*

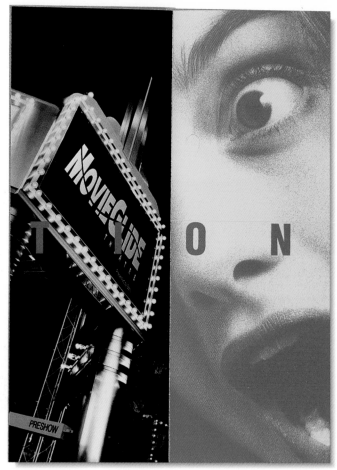

CLARION BUSINESS COMMUNICATIONS *SONY ENTERTAINMENT SYSTEMS*

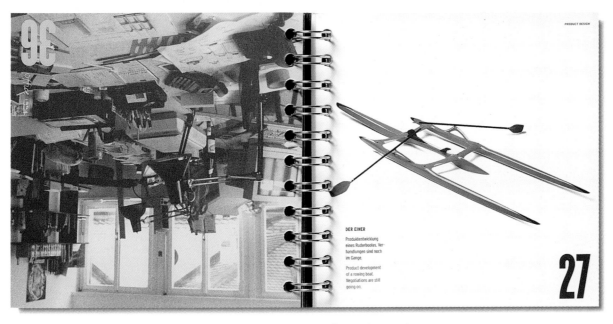

HUG, VON MOOS & DORFMÜLLER *(IN-HOUSE)*

SIEGER DESIGN (IN-HOUSE)

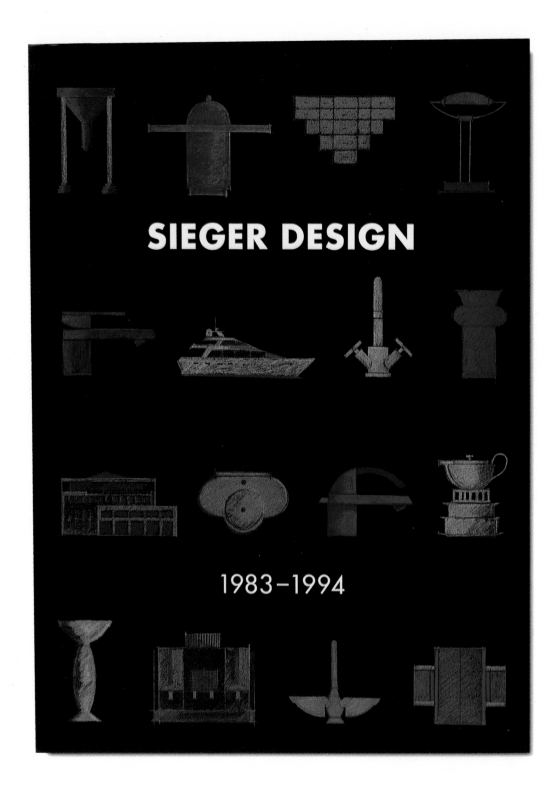

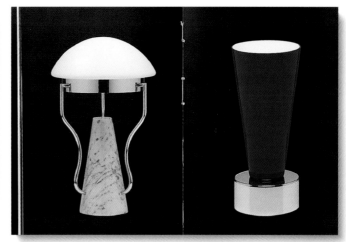

FONTANA

Waschtisch *washstand*
Alape **1987**

Zeugleich mit der »Metamorphosen«-
Armatur wurde der »Fontana«-Brunnen
als modernes Zitat klassischer römischer
Brunnen entworfen. Bestehend aus
einem schlichten runden Becken, von
vier verchromten Säulen getragen, ist
»Fontana« ein Waschtisch, der durch
seine skulpturale Erscheinung geprägt
wird. So nimmt auch der Spiegel mit
dem emaillierten Bogen ein Element
klassischer Architektur auf.

*The »Fontana« fountain was designed at
the same time as the »Metamorphosen« fit-
ting as a modern quotation of classic
Roman fountains. It consists of a plain,
round basin supported by four chromium-
plated columns, making it a washstand
with a markedly sculptural appearance.
The mirror with its enamelled arch picks
up an element of classical architecture as
well.*

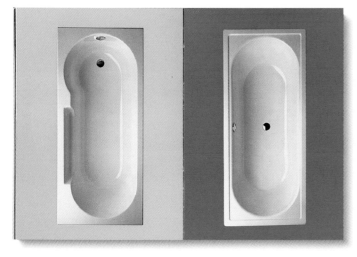

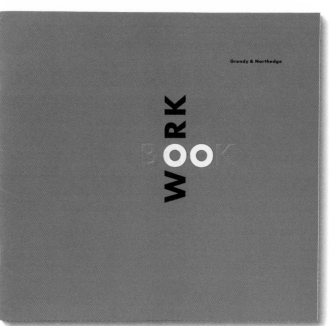

GRUNDY & NORTHEDGE (*IN-HOUSE*)

LARSON DESIGN *(IN-HOUSE)*

MÄRTTERER + SCHUSCHKLEB GMBH *(IN-HOUSE)*

Parallèle

Notre mission consiste à créer, dans le cadre d'une relation de confiance établie dès les premiers instants, des instruments de communication qui suscitent une perception positive et durable de nos clients, de leurs produits et de leurs services. Notre force repose sur des ressources humaines et technologiques de haut calibre, qui œuvrent de concert à l'atteinte des objectifs de nos clients, à l'intérieur de deux disciplines fusionnées dans un processus unique:

la **communication-design**.

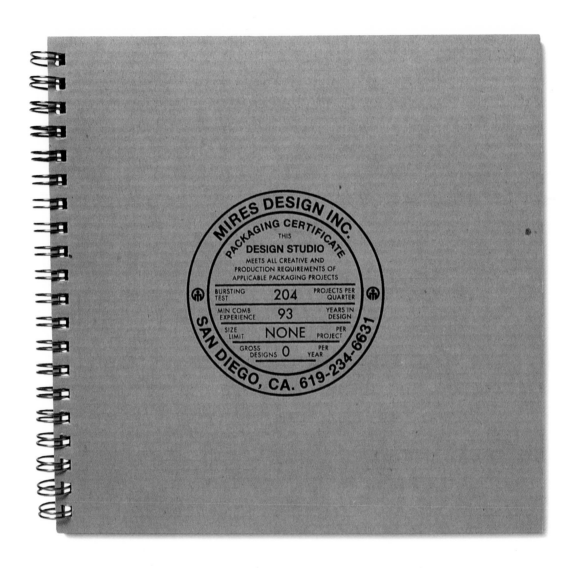

MIRES DESIGN *(IN-HOUSE)*

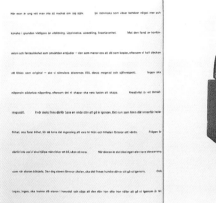

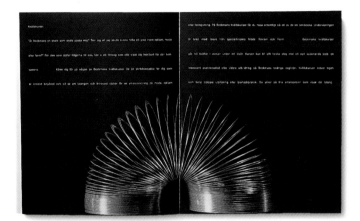

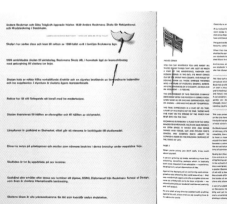

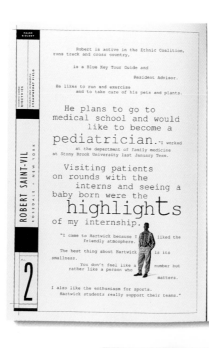

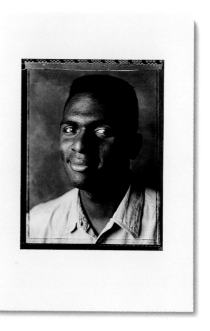

Tamara is president of the International Club and a member of Beta Beta Beta, the biology honor society. "I love studying other languages—English, Italian, French; skiing; reading fiction; and laying out in the sun at Pine Lake. It's great going to the lake with my friends on a beautiful spring day.

Her favorite Hartwick tradition is Wick Wars, a sort of wacky Olympics held during Spring Weekend. "Nothing seems to be as exciting and thrilling as participating in the Wick Wars!!

"I came to Hartwick because I wanted to go to a small private college with a strong biology department. Hartwick was a perfect match when I graduate I would like to gain experience in medical research and later go to medical school. My dream since childhood was to become a doctor and I will do everything to reach my goal."

TAMARA CHIGOGIDZE
TBILISI · GEORGIA · CIS

No. 7

FRANK B. PANZARELLA JR.
GLENDORA · NEW JERSEY

No. 12

I t's hard to imagine how he does it all. Frank plays varsity football, is the Computer Club treasurer and a computer trainer for computer services. He's also active in the Student Union Programming Board. Plus he likes competition archery, hunting, snow skiing, water skiing, weightlifting and many other sports; restores classic cars; plays the saxophone; and loves Broadway plays and reading.

"I came to Hartwick because of the small size, low student-to-faculty ratio and strong liberal arts curriculum. I also was attracted by the beauty of the campus and surrounding area and the friendly atmosphere on campus. The best thing about Hartwick is the personal touch you get by being on a first-name basis with your professors. You are not just another face in a crowded classroom."

As a result of a January Term internship at Oneonta's A.O. Fox Memorial Hospital, Frank plans to attend graduate school and earn an M.B.A. in health-care/hospital administration or management of information systems.

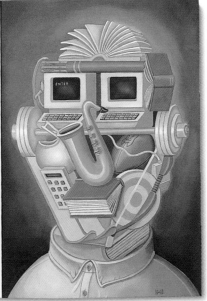

AMY ROWE
PHOENIX · ARIZONA

No. 14

AMY IS ON THE SWIM TEAM AND LIKES PHOTOGRAPHY, ART, MUSIC AND READING NOVELS. "MY FAVORITE SPOT IN ONEONTA IS THE FARMLAND DIRECTLY TO THE SOUTH OF CAMPUS ON THE MOUNTAIN BECAUSE IT IS SO BEAUTIFUL. ✕ "I CAME TO HARTWICK BECAUSE I HAD THE OPPORTUNITY TO SWIM ON A GOOD TEAM AND TO GO TO A SCHOOL ON THE OTHER SIDE OF THE COUNTRY. I GET TO EXPERIENCE A DIFFERENT PACE OF LIFE HERE. I HAVE GROWN IN MY OWN INDEPENDENCE AND RESPONSIBILITY." ✕ SHE ENJOYS GOING TO THE SOCCER GAMES AND RELISHES THE GREAT FAN SUPPORT. "I SEE THE SAME COMPETITIVE EDGE DISPLAYED BY OUR SOCCER TEAM THAT I HAVE IN MY SWIMMING." ✕ "THE BEST THING ABOUT HARTWICK IS THE WIDE RANGE OF OFF-CAMPUS STUDY PROGRAMS. THE JANUARY TERM TRIPS TAKE STUDENTS TO PLACES THEY MAY NEVER HAVE THE OPPORTUNITY TO TRAVEL TO ON THEIR OWN. I AM REALLY LOOKING FORWARD TO MY FIRST TRIP. WHEN I GRADUATE I WOULD LIKE TO GO INTO THE PEACE CORPS FOR A FEW YEARS AND THEN COME BACK TO THE UNITED STATES AND FIND A JOB THAT I AM INTERESTED IN AND THAT MAKES ME HAPPY."

RUTKA WEADOCK DESIGN *Hartwick College*

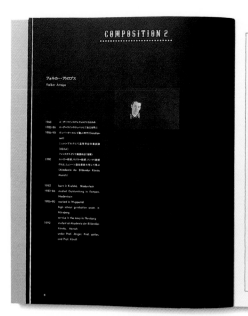

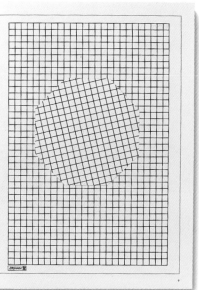

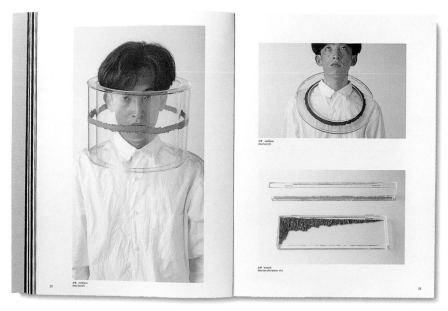

B-BI STUDIO INC. *HIKOMIZUNO COLLEGE OF JEWELRY*

CRONAN DESIGN *CALIFORNIA COLLEGE OF ARTS AND CRAFTS*

MICHAEL PETERS GROUP *ART CENTER COLLEGE OF DESIGN—EUROPE*

RUTKA WEADOCK DESIGN *Hartwick College*

ART CENTER COLLEGE OF DESIGN (EUROPE)

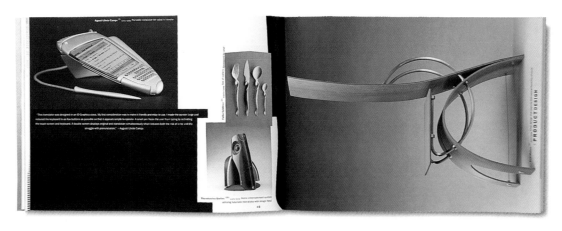

ART CENTER COLLEGE OF DESIGN-EUROPE (IN-HOUSE)

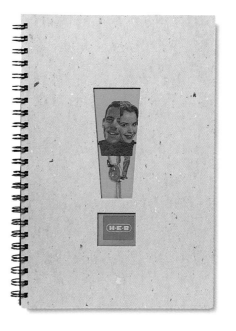

THE NORTH CHARLES STREET DESIGN ORGANIZATION *THE UNIVERSITY OF MISSOURI–COLUMBIA*

The
Brooklyn Academy of Music
1995
Next
Wave
Festival

BAM's 1995 Next Wave
Festival is sponsored by
Philip Morris Companies Inc.

PENTAGRAM DESIGN *BROOKLYN ACADEMY OF MUSIC*

THE
PENGUIN
IS
ADMIRABLY
SUITED
FOR
WET,
COLD
WEATHER.

THE
HUMAN
IS
NOT.

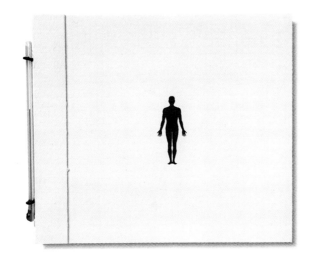

THE
PENGUIN
HAS A THICK COAT
OF
WATER-
PROOF
FEATHERS.

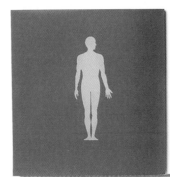

THE
HUMAN
DOES
NOT.

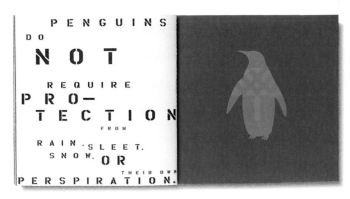

PENGUINS
DO
NOT
REQUIRE
PRO-
TECTION
FROM
RAIN. SLEET.
SNOW. OR
THEIR OWN
PERSPIRATION.

HUMANS
DO.

BE OUR GUEST IN THE PENGUIN HOUSE
AT THE CENTRAL PARK WILDLIFE CENTER.
830 FIFTH AVE. (AT 64TH ST.) ON TUESDAY,
MAY 9TH AT 6:00 P.M. TO WELCOME
STORM·F.I.T.™ FABRIC – THE NEWEST MEMBER
OF THE PERFORMANCE LINE OF NIKE F.I.T.
FABRICS – INTO THE WORLD. PLEASE R.S.V.P.
TO LIZ FLYNN AT 212.505.9494.

[WARM CAPS WILL BE PROVIDED.]

NIKE, INC. (IN-HOUSE)

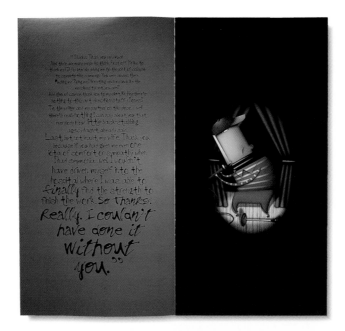

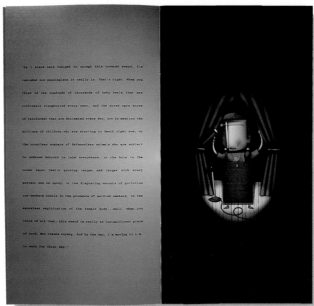

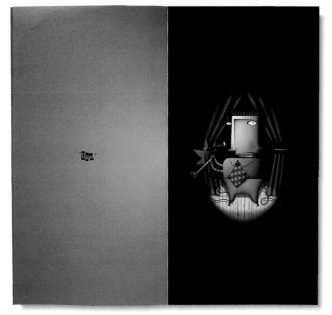

PIERSON HAWKINS INC. ADVERTISING *DENVER ADVERTISING FEDERATION*

ROBERT TALBOTT
NECKWEAR REMAINS
THE MOST ELEGANT OF
GENTLEMEN'S ACCESSORIES:
HANDSOME, WELL-MADE AND QUITE
AFFORDABLE. THE UNSURPASSED QUALITY OF
ROBERT TALBOTT NECKTIES BESPEAKS TRADITION
AND REFINEMENT: A QUIET ASSURANCE WITH REMARKABLE
POWERS OF SUGGESTION. FROM THE SPIRITED CLASSICS OF THE
BEST OF CLASS COLLECTION TO THE AUDACIOUS PRINTS OF OUR
EXCLUSIVE OMAGGIO SERIES, TALBOTT OFFERS AN ARRAY OF SUPPLE

THE TALBOTT SHIRT

NATURAL FINISHED WITTY DAPPER HANDSOME

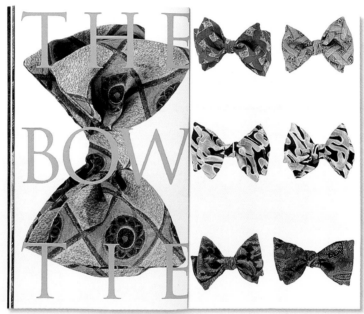

THE BOW TIE

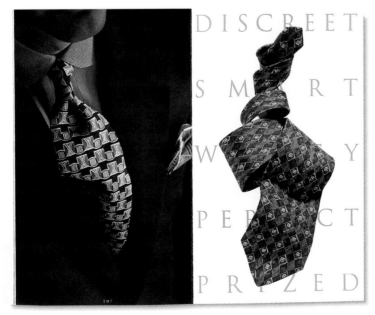

DISCREET SMART WITTY PERFECT PRIZED

VANDERBYL DESIGN *ROBERT TALBOTT, INC.*

PLATE TWO

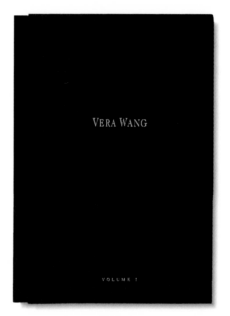

VERA WANG

VOLUME 1

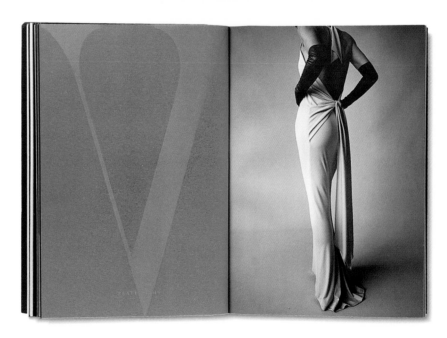

PLATE THREE

PLATE FIFTEEN | PLATE SIXTEEN

SOCIO X *Vera Wang*

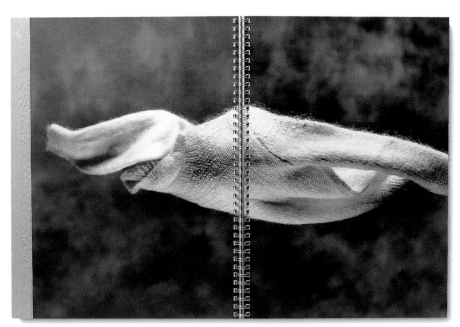

NEIMAN MARCUS *(IN-HOUSE)*

COMPOSURE IS SOMETHING YOU RADIATE, AS OPPOSED TO SOMETHING YOU PUT ON.

DOUBLE RL BY RALPH LAUREN... as worn by Malcolm McLaren, composer

VERSACE CLASSIC... as worn by Tevin Campbell, singer

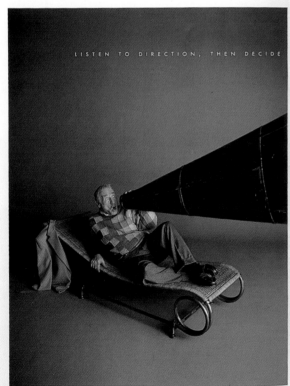

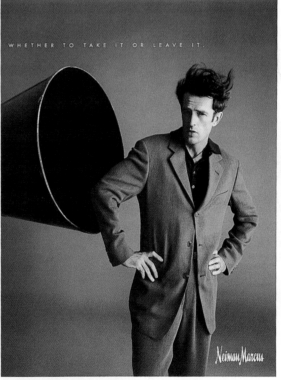

LISTEN TO DIRECTION, THEN DECIDE WHETHER TO TAKE IT OR LEAVE IT.

NM EXCLUSIVE CASHMERE... as worn by Mel Brooks, director

DONNA KARAN... as worn by Rupert Everett, actor

NEIMAN MARCUS *(IN-HOUSE)*

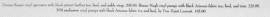

Donna Karan vinyl spectator with black patent leather toe, heel, and ankle strap, 295.00. Bruno Magli vinyl pumps with black Arianna fabric toe, heel, and trim, 225.00. NM exclusive vinyl pumps with black Arianna fabric toe and heel, by Yves Saint Laurent, 165.00.

Both by Calvin Klein, of brown lizard-embossed leather: Multi-banded sandal with stacked heel, 220.00. Open-toe sandal with high heel, 250.00.

Via Spiga golden leather strappy mule in white cushioned insole, 110.00.

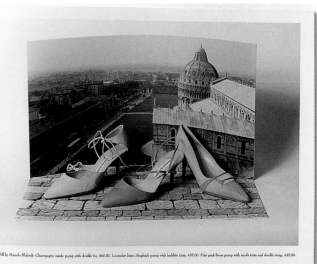

All by Manolo Blahnik: Champagne suede pump with double tie, 465.00. Lavender linen slingback pump with kidskin trim, 455.00. Pale pink linen pump with suede trim and double strap, 435.00.

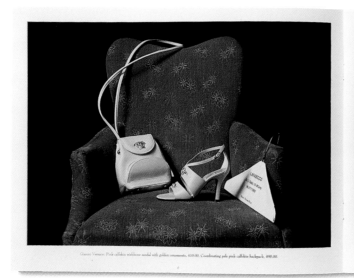

Gianni Versace. Pink calfskin wishbone sandal with golden ornaments, 410.00. Coordinating pale pink calfskin backpack, 495.00.

Un amore a prima vista

DKNY patent leather high-heel mule with buckled straps, in red (shown), black, or white, 165.00.

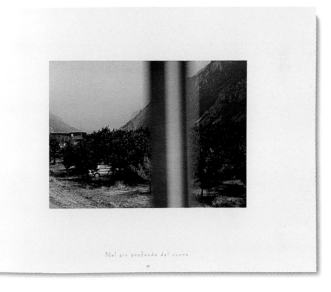

Nel più profondo del cuore

Philippe Model elastic mules with black stacked heel, in fuchsia or black, 165.00.

Both by Charles Jourdan La Collection: Leather tie pumps, in pale pink or taupe, 195.00. Pearlized leather slingback pump, in mauve (shown) or taupe, 185.00.

NEIMAN MARCUS *(IN-HOUSE)*

ZIMMERMANN CROWE DESIGN *LEVI STRAUSS & CO.*

TAILGATE

SLAUGHTER-HANSON *PLAINCLOTHES*

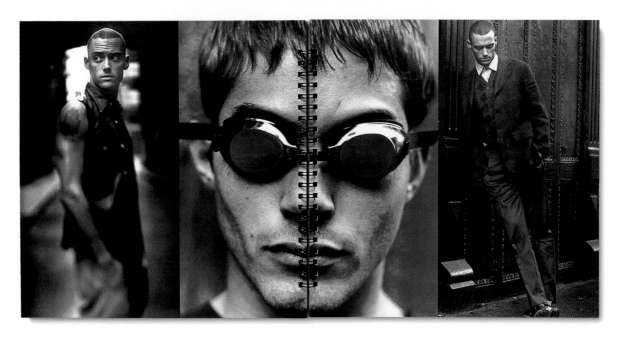

LISKA AND ASSOCIATES *AMERICAN CREW*

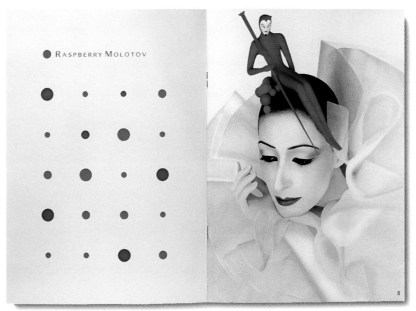

SHISEIDO COMPANY, LTD. (*IN-HOUSE*)

KARLA COLLETTO

POLLARD CREATIVE *Karla Colletto*

Amsterdam, Anvers, Atlanta, Baden-Baden, Bangkok, Basel, Berlin, Bern, Beverly Hills, Bonn, Bordeaux, Boston, Bruxelles, Buenos Aires, Cannes, Chicago, Dallas, Davos, Den Haag, Dubai, Dublin, Edinburgh, Genève, Hannover, Helsinki, Hong Kong, Interlaken, Jakarta, Jeddah, Köln, Kuala Lumpur, London, Lisboa, Lugano, Luxembourg, Luzern, Lyon, Marseille, Melbourne, Mexico, Monte Carlo, Montreal, Montreux, München, New York, Nice, Osaka, Oxford, Paris, Riyadh, Rotterdam, Salzburg, San Francisco, Santiago de Chile, Scottsdale, Shanghai, Shenzhen, Singapore, St. Moritz, Stockholm, Sydney, Taipei, Tokyo, Toronto, Washington, Wien, Zürich.

PERSONNE NE SE DONNE LA PEINE DE REGARDER CES TABLEAUX AVEC BIENVEILLANCE, DE LES INTERROGER. CHACUN VEUT Y RETROUVER LE REFLET DE SA PETITE ÂME. PERSONNE NE SE DONNE LA PEINE D'EXAMINER LES NOUVEAUX MOYENS D'EXPRESSION. CE SONT EUX QUI POURTANT OUVRENT LA VOIE À L'ART MODERNE.

SEILER DDB BERNE *BALLY MANAGEMENT AG*

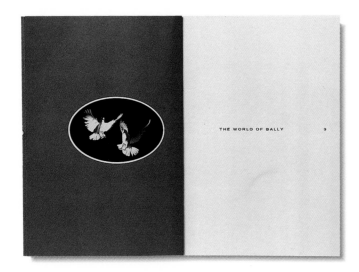

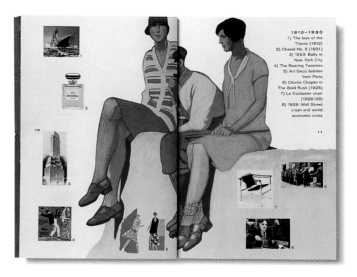

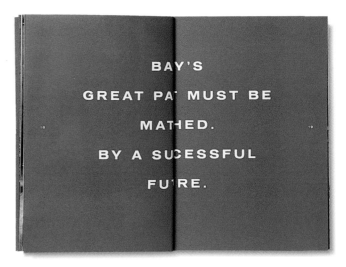

SEILER DDB BERNE *Bally Management AG*

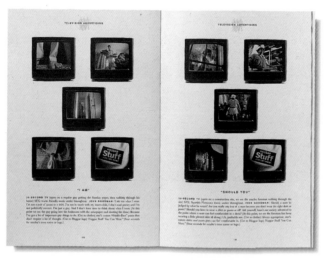

GOODBY, SILVERSTEIN & PARTNERS *Haggar Clothing Co.*

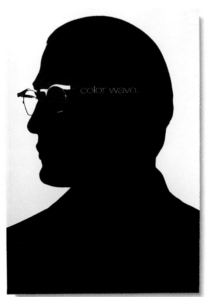

LUNETTES ROBERT LA ROCHE (*IN-HOUSE*)

Richard Tyler

She

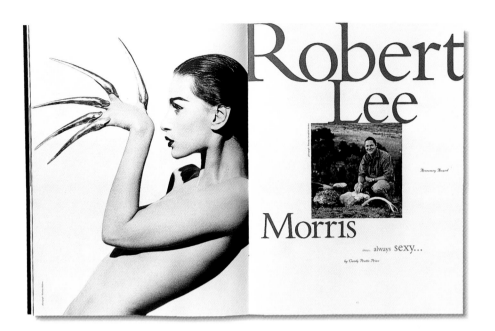

Robert Lee Morris

...always sexy...

by Candy Pratts Price

Accessory Award

Is there anyone in the fashion world who doesn't know

Lifetime Achievement

Bernadine Morris?

You would see her always seated in the front row at runway shows, her cap of silvery hair gleaming under the lights, her eyes hidden by wood-framed glasses, her pen making neat shorthand notes in a spiral-bound notebook. You would avidly read her reviews in *The New York Times* the next day to see which designers rated a rave and which didn't rate a line. *But did you know...*

She was the *fastest* gun in the fashion game, tossing off those insightful, elegantly written reviews in less than an hour? She could be kind to a designer's mistakes but was once known to reduce an *editor* to tears? Her favorite place for lunch — after Le Cirque — was *The Times cafeteria*? The reason she didn't return phone calls was that she didn't know *how* to retrieve her Voice Mail? She was a *corset* editor at Women's Wear Daily? She once defied a *stewardess* to take away her cigarette on a plane? She often bought her *pantyhose* at the five-and-ten? She was a *ping*-pong champion? She wore an authentic Chinese workman's suit to a party at Yves Saint Laurent's home — and left a stain of blue dye on his *white* sofa? Her weekend home is not in a *chic* Hampton but in Baiting Hollow? What you all *do* know is that Bernadine has always been the most unpretentious, unfashiony fashion writer in the business. Oh, she'll do herself up in Scaasi or de la Renta when the occasion demands, but her favorite mode of dress is a sweater, pants and comfortable shoes. Always comfortable shoes. It may be because Bernadine is a writer first, and a fashion writer second. She says she really wanted to be a foreign correspondent, and that may help to explain her lean, precise prose style and her calmness under pressure. If you ask her how she could keep writing about the same designer's collections season after season, year after year, she would tell you she reads the sports pages. Her theory is if you could find a fresh way to write about a baseball game, you could find a fresh way to write about a fashion show. She doesn't want to write about fashion shows any more. But, lucky for us, she doesn't plan to give up writing. See you on the sports pages, Bernadine?

by Anne-Marie Schiro

Jackie

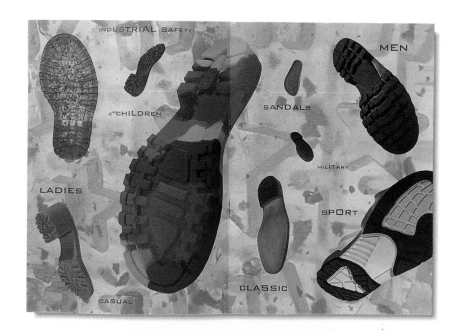

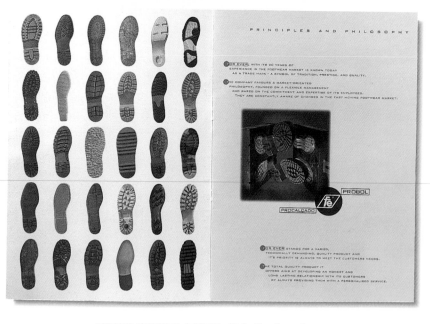

ANTERO FERREIRA DESIGN, LDA. *FOR EVER GROUP*

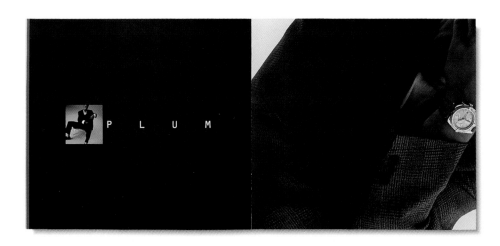

TERRELONGE *Elite Model Management Toronto*

UNRESERVED SEATING   WIELAND FURNITURE   available worldwide

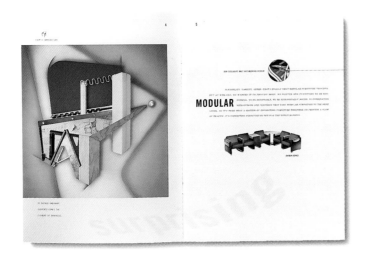

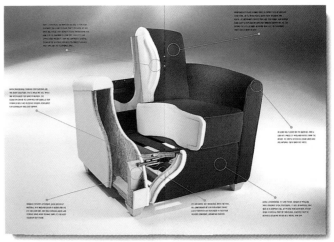

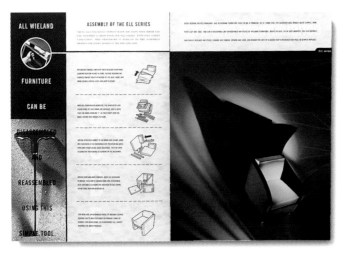

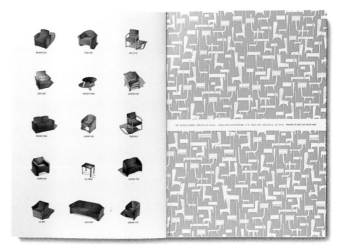

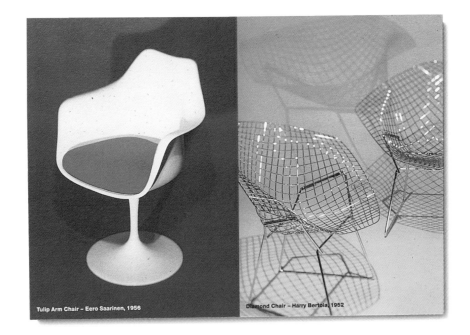

Tulip Arm Chair – Eero Saarinen, 1956

Diamond Chair – Harry Bertoia, 1952

Knoll is honored to have **thirty** of its designs in the **Design** Collection of The Museum of **Modern Art.** Here are just a few.

Coffee Table – Florence Knoll, 1954

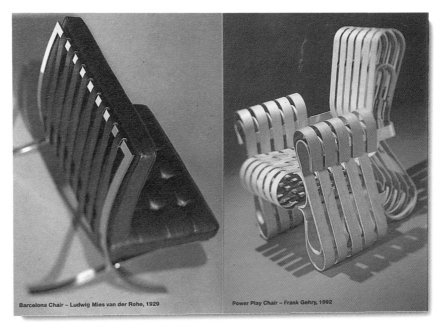

Barcelona Chair – Ludwig Mies van der Rohe, 1929

Power Play Chair – Frank Gehry, 1992

KNOLL GRAPHICS *KNOLL*

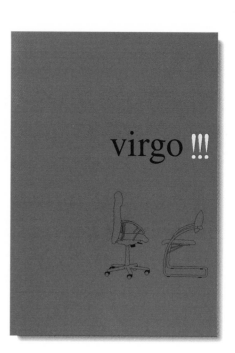

URS V. SCHWERZMANN *ELKA GMBH*

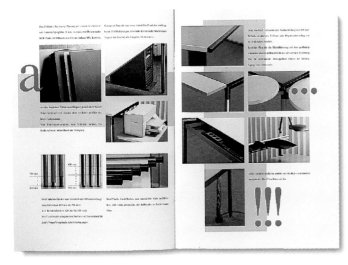

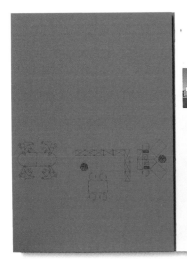

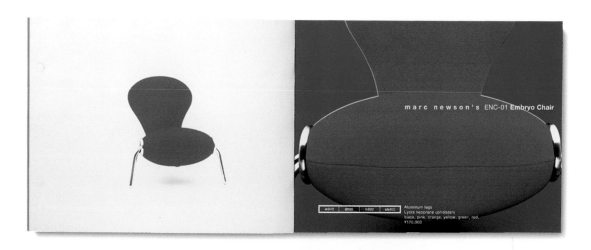

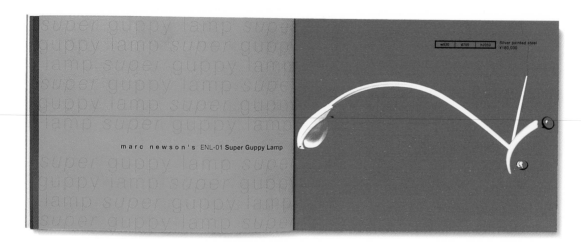

SUSAN MORIGUCHI *IDEE CO., LTD.*

all the best

JONES STUDIO LIMITED *M2L*

REUNION is elegant furniture for executive offices that marries tra-

ditional detailing and timeless design. This full wood line includes

Mitered edge mold-
ings are classic in
style and are accent-
ed by a fine, linear
polished brass or
black reveal.

desks and credenzas, bookcases and

breakfronts, conference tables and

Workwall: a HANDSOME alternative to custom-made wood storage and

worksurfaces for executive spaces. All are

A pull-out worksurface
provides additional
space at the desk
when it's needed, dis-
appears into the wood-
work when it's not.
Invisible integral side
pulls are standard.
(Traditional brass pulls
are an option).

distinguished by Reunion's signature edge

moldings and subtle brass or black reveal. Reunion is HANDCRAFTED

of prime cherry hardwood and matched veneers. Every suite is assem-

Pedestal drawers have
full-extension black
glides, accommodate
letter and legal files.
Expanded storage per-
mits two-deep filing of
letter-size folders.

bled by a single craftsman to ensure per-

fect fit. And following fit there's FINISH —

cherry, mahogany and walnut finishes hand rubbed to a radiant lustre.

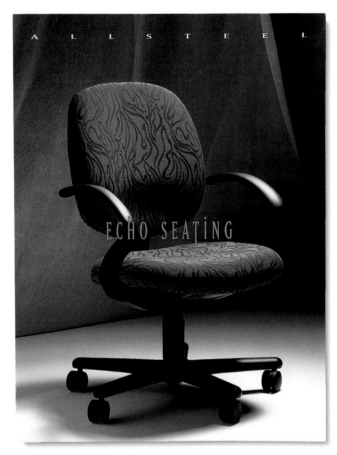

GIBBS BARONET *ALLSTEEL*

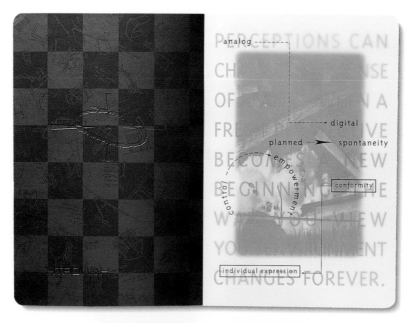

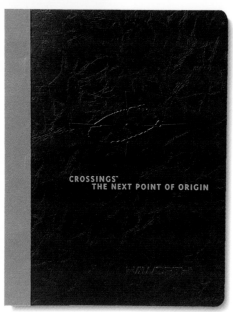

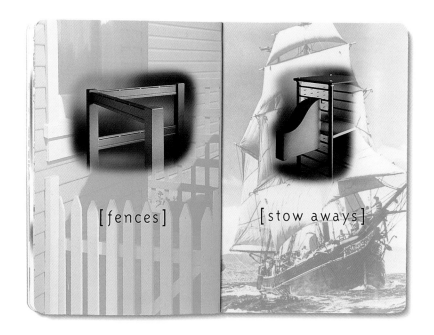

[fences] [stow aways]

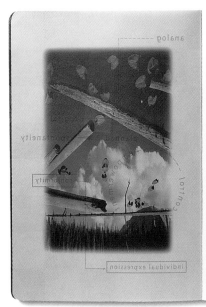

PERCEPTIONS CAN CHANGE YOUR SENSE OF REALITY. WHEN A FRESH PERSPECTIVE BECOMES A NEW BEGINNING, THE WAY YOU VIEW YOUR ENVIRONMENT CHANGES FOREVER.

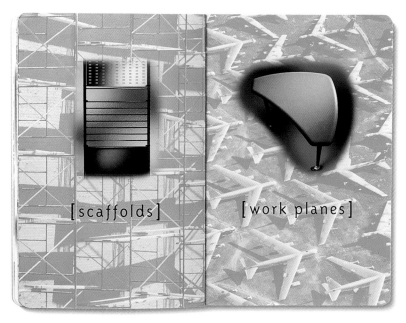

[scaffolds] [work planes]

THE DAWSON & COMPANY CREATIVE GROUP *Haworth, Inc.*

CRAIG FRAZIER

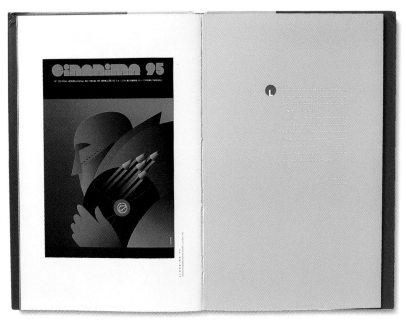

JOÃO MACHADO

(Opposite Top) **LOUEY/RUBINO DESIGN GROUP** *Le Bar Bat*
(Opposite Middle) **ROGERS SEIDMAN DESIGN TEAM** *Campagna Restaurant*
(Opposite Bottom) **LOUEY/RUBINO DESIGN GROUP** *Zen Palate*
(This Page) **DENNARD CREATIVE INC.** *Bennigan's Restaurants*

CONTENTS

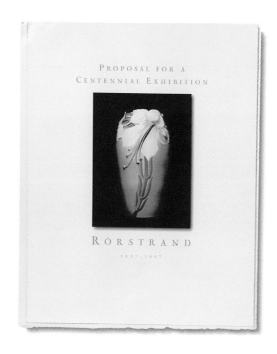

CENTENNIAL EXHIBITION

The Stockholm exhibition of 1897 was an important event in Rörstrand's history. Turn of the century Europe was alive with change as young artists were rebelling against their Victorian upbringing. Encouragement came from writers like Ellen Key who criticized popular heavy-handed ornamentation and challenged the artistic community to bring beauty and simplicity into the home with everyday objects.

Robert Almströom, Rörstrand's director took the challenge seriously and hired several young artists in 1895 and 1896, aiming his sights toward the Stockholm exhibition of 1897. The exhibition opened on May 15th to overwhelming response as Rörstrand's new artists exhibited their designs among the traditional patterns. Rörstrand's success at this exhibition marked the beginning of a new era for the company, recognized today as its Art Nouveau Period.

At the Paris exhibition of 1900, Rörstrand once again received enormous praise. It was here that Rörstrand developed an international reputation for excellence in the company of Gallé, Tiffany, and Sèvres. The proposed exhibition will commemorate the Stockholm exhibition of 1897 and the Paris exhibition of 1900, a century after these events. The touring exhibition will once again present Rörstrand's Art Nouveau porcelain to the public.

The traveling exhibition will include many important examples of Rörstrand from a private collection, as well as significant pieces from museum and corporate collections. The exhibition includes the works of Rörstrand's artistic elite: Alf Wallander, Nils Lundström, Algot Eriksson, Karl and Waldemar Linderlöm, Anna Boberg, and Astrid Fwezlöf.

The book, *Rörstrand Porcelain: Art Nouveau Masterpieces*, will serve as the catalog for the exhibition and encourage museum participation.

STOCKHOLM EXHIBITION OF 1897

CONTRIBUTIONS

In order for Exhibitions International to begin the process of coordinating a touring exhibition, some funding is required. There are numerous ways to be involved and the marketing department of the sponsor could determine the scope of participation.

Museums, as you may know, schedule exhibitions well in advance, so the planning process should begin shortly. More details can be made available.

CONCLUSION

The costs associated with the publication of the book have already been absorbed, and a major portion of the exhibition funding will be offset through museum participation fees.

By underwriting the organisational costs in circulating this exhibition, the sponsor could take full advantage of this marketing opportunity in North America and Europe.

SOCIO X *ROBERT SCHREIBER*

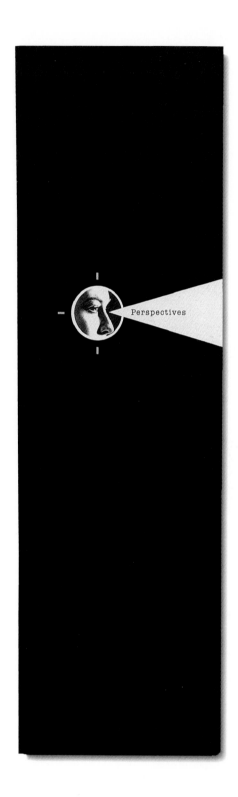

Perspectives

ends with a gallery

featuring a changing

selection of works

from the past decade.

Changing every three

months, these

exhibitions-

within-an-exhibition

explore aspects of

recent and current art

practice.

[ENJOY]

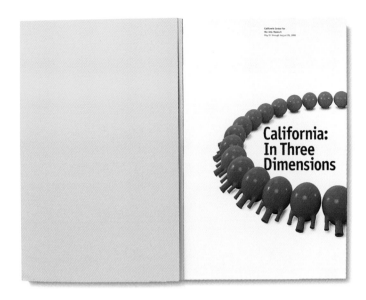

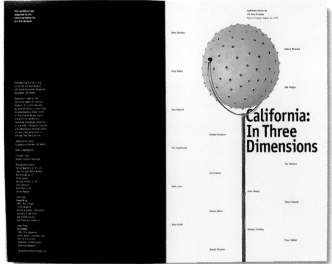

James Turrell or the Plexiglas wall forms of Craig Kaufman), they do find color and comfort in the terrain between two and three dimensional form.

We are most indebted to Mary Bates, Rob Craigie, Tom Driscoll, Mineko Grimmer, Tim Hawkinson, Tina Hulett, Jay Johnson, Mark Lere, Anne Mudge, Tomas Nakada, Minoru Ohira, Ross Rudel, Peter Shelton, Melissa Smedley, Robert Therrien, Peter Walker, and Daniel Wheeler who have explored the connections and boundaries between painting and sculpture in abstract and semi-abstract work and have shared their ideas, strategies, and objects.

While everyone on the museum staff had some part in this exhibition, Curatorial Assistant Catherine Gleason wove its many threads together into a workable whole.

Reesey Shaw, Director

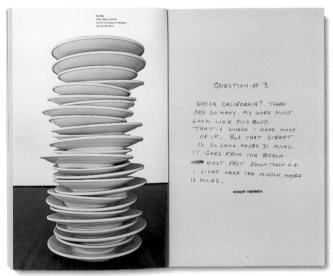

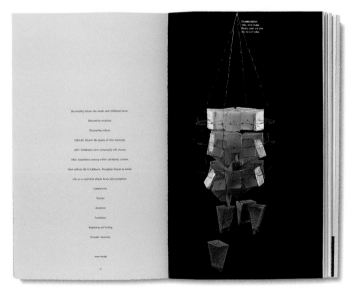

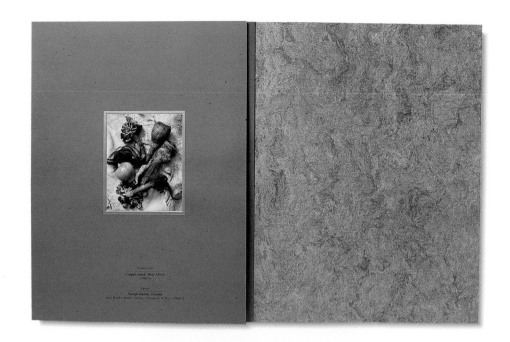

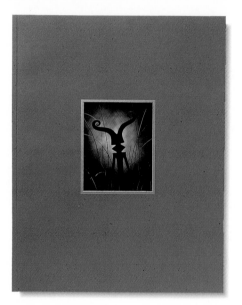

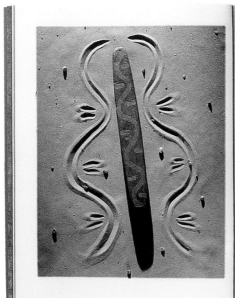

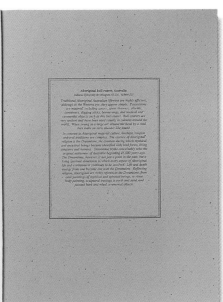

Aboriginal bull-roarer, Australia

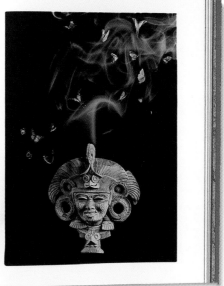

Ceramic mask from a ritual censer, Teotihuacan, Mexico

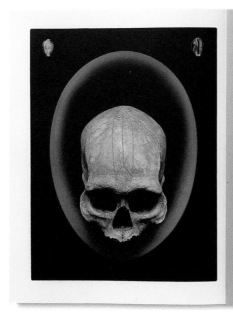

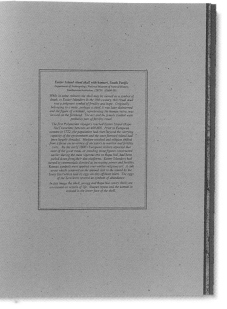

Easter Island ritual skull with komari, South Pacific

WOOD/BROD DESIGN *Corson Hirschfeld/The Hennegan Company*

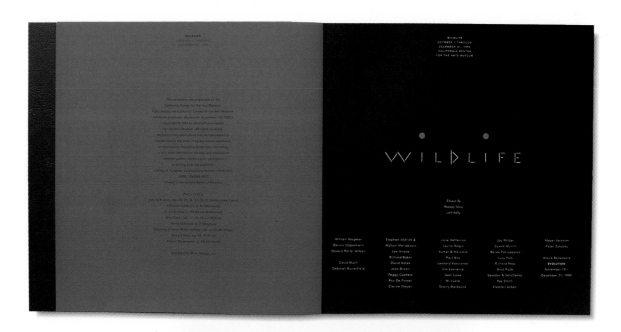

WILLIAM WEGMAN

Photographer, painter and video artist William Wegman, with his Weimaraner pets Man Ray, Fay Ray and Battina, has made a career of inventing and documenting the antics of his dogs. In 1970 when Wegman bought his first dog, Man Ray, as a pet, he had no idea that the pup would wander into his photo shoots and insist on being "part of the action." At some point, it became easier for the photographer to incorporate the dog into his work than to lure him out.

The black and white early 1970s images of Man Ray changed by the end of the decade to the brilliantly colored grainless images produced by a new Polaroid 20" x 24" camera. It is these Polaroids of more recent pets, Fay Ray and Battie, from Wegman's personal collection that are the first creatures of **Wildlife**. • In the 1970s Wegman began to dress Man Ray in costumes. With these outfits, and later with elaborate sets, the dog began to assume human behaviors: in bed watching TV, wearing nail polish, and in a canoe in Indian headdress. • In a continual parade of images from elegant abstractions with the dog posed on cubes to familiar narratives like the fairy tales **Cinderella** and **Little Red Riding Hood**, Wegman's dogs are human surrogates. Their doleful gaze as they participate in the rituals of our species—marriage ceremonies, housekeeping, and preening in front of a mirror—inspire both humor and self reflection. Somehow two dogs lying in bed together, their paws draped over the fold of the covers intently watching TV, makes

a stronger statement about our culture than people depicted in the same pose ever could. • Wegman lets the dogs play themselves and thus selects them for roles based on their own personalities. The artist thinks that dogs are the only animals that care about people, and is painfully aware that he will experience the loss of six generations of caring dogs in his lifetime. He watches and documents as the puppy becomes the adolescent, then all too quickly reaches maturity and progresses to old age. • After 23 years of working with dogs, Wegman's collaboration with his animals is such that he can conspire with them to imitate a sweet grandmother or a vicious wolf. Recent book projects include **ABC** and **1,2,3**-in which the dogs' bodies are arranged to form letters and numbers. • The dogs will assume super sleuth poses in **The Hardly Boys**, a spoof on the boys' mystery series of the 1940s. • Fay Ray and Battie come to their master and ask him to play with them. Since their master is Wegman, the "playing" becomes art.

DENNIS OPPENHEIM

The artistic life of sculptor Dennis Oppenheim is marked by variety. His pioneering projects in the 1960s and 1970s include performance and conceptual works as well as process pieces that investigate his own body and the landscape. If any thread can be found in the disparate forms of Oppenheim's oeuvre it is his feverish search for the roots of transformation–alchemical formulas that make lightning strike, teeth chatter, and send the stuff of this world flying into the

air. The six deer that circle the gallery to form 1993's **Digestion: Gypsum Gypsies** began as a single animal. For the artist the antlers of the deer seemed to want to become a candelabra–yet this alteration did not suggest a familiar species, but one the artist invents to explore ideas of time, mutation, and metaphysical power. • In another permutation of **Digestion**, the four flaming deer were bisected and attached to the walls of the gallery–seeming to appear and disappear through the plasterboard. The artist thought of the animals as "gypsum gypsies" that were both digesting the wall and drawing energy from it. The flaming horns suggest that the bodies of the animals are furnaces that can "breathe fire" like a dragon. This alchemical transformation adds a performance component to the static form and allows the animals to become an armature for Oppenheim's ideas about the violence of change, the vacillation between

life and death, abstraction, real time, and the deep-rooted psychological states suggested by heat and danger. • In this most recent (1993) permutation of **Digestion**, the six deer are no longer attached to the wall but circle the gallery and confront each other. Several seem to paw the ground with heads down as they tilt their fiery antlers. • A lineage can be traced back to Oppenheim's work with live animals in the 1970s (a parrot, a dog, a tarantula), but this recent **Digestion** is less transactional and more removed from real time. It exemplifies the artist's need to continually find a blank slate and create a mystique that challenges life's mysteries rather than establishing a signature style. It is in this quest for magic that Oppenheim finds the psychic strength to threaten his art-historical position, face life's challenges, and create action-oriented works that throb.

WILLIAM WEGMAN
INNUENDO CHAIR, 1990
POLAROID
24 X 20 INCHES

DONALD FOLLER-WILSON
*COOKIE WANTED IT...MISS TEXAS—
THE CROWN...BUT...WEG GOT IT...MISS
TEXAS—THE CROWN!...*, 1992/93
OIL ON TWO PANELS
21 1/2 X 18 INCHES EACH

WILDLIFE by JEFF KELLEY

When I was in high school only girls drew horses. I drew the skull of a steer, tak-ing four months to account for its every weathered crack and bony flake. It was dry and minimal, like the desert landscape of southern Nevada where I lived. It had metaphorical distance—it was cool—because of its deadness. While the skull was drawn in the style of Andrew Wyeth, its sensibility was of the inert, industrial and natural materials then being used by minimalist sculptors and land artists of whom I was only vaguely aware. (Later, in art school, Robert Smithson would become *my* hero.) Horses were girl art. • Looking back, my anti-horse bias was indicative of broader cultural biases about the proper subject matter of art at the time. As a young artist, my sense of nature was of its esthetic abstractions: of its space, time, process, materiality, light, and so on. It was an empirical resource for artists. "Nature" in its more figural incarna-tions—like animals—was thought to be sentimental, unworthy of serious artistic activity. The romanticism it evoked was to be avoided at all costs. One result was that while I steered clear of horses I also subordinated all other wildlife

in my unconscious hierarchy of esthetic subject matter. Our subjects—"space," "surface," "color," "paint"—had to be like our objects, and while this reduction of terms was among the par-ticular contributions of Minimalism to American art, it nonetheless tended to limit the range of permissible subjects for artists. Like the human figure in painting and sculpture around 1970, animals were out of style. • Then I saw my first Deborah Butterfield horses. Composed of twisted, corrugated tin or woven of sticks and mud, they were among the most poetic things I'd ever seen. They seemed suspended between esthetic categories: were they sculptures, drawings in space, or, when in groups of two

or three, installations (herds)? Because of this ambiguity, as well as their real life scale, they fell back upon some essential identifi-cation with their subject matter-horses. You didn't have to squint at the "art" to see its meaning or feel its presence. Some quality of horseness was held inside them like a spirit. It was so palpable that you hesitated to get too close, half-wondering if the things would move. • Like debris washed up along the edge of a creek after the flood waters recede, Butterfield's horses have a residual presence. They represent what's left after the artist's encounter with the landscape where she finds the parts that will compose them. All their sticks and straw and scrap metal seem held in a

his turkeys are what Jim Lewis calls "antitotems," the purpose of which is to deny the sense of cultural and psychological place—one's sense of identity—that totems (and other cultural fetishes) are meant to foster. These are not about animals, or even systems of animal classification. They are semiotic turkeys, parodies of cultural identity, and might be understood as a critique of multiculturalism as a "postmodern" form of tribal classification. As Lewis puts it, "there are no natural kinds." • Well, I'm not so sure. I think what this show suggests is that there are countless natural kinds, and that it continues to be a mistake to believe that we are not among them. Sure, cultural identity is a slippery issue these days, but that does not automatically make turkeys into human signifiers. The larger question is not whether we—animals all—are natural, but whether naturalness is a human-centered value that no longer applies. When used as a term that justifies unchecked human "progress" in the eco-sphere, nature, a purely cultural ideal, is just another form of global violence. It remains crucial that we stop seeing nature and culture as opposites in a dialectical pair, for the dialogue between them has proven to be an unbalanced monologue—a rhetoric of human dominion over the earth. • Rather, it is the interdependence of culture and nature that most of the artists in **Wildlife** seem to be thinking about in their various depictions of animals. This kind of thinking is also a feature of what has lately been termed "eco-feminism," and reminds me once again of my adolescent estimations of "girl art." In retrospect, it was the girls more than the boys of

my generation who made the greatest impact upon the arts. With feminism, a new wave of human "nature," which under-stood its connection to culture and politics, was unleashed. Its energies—sometimes destructive, sometimes preservational—opened up closed systems of thought and action, much as the Wild Animal Park of Escondido—and places like it—helped open up Victorian ideas of "the zoo." In this opening up, our relation-ships with nature and its "other" citizens have slowly begun to change. • Expressed in those changing relationships are some of the most compelling and significant ethical and envi-ronmental dilemmas of the late twentieth century, contests for rights and resources that foreshadow those of the century to come. The questions of animal life, consciousness, and habitat are central to our changing perspectives of ourselves as members, but not rulers, of the planet. Moving from an ego-centered, anthropocentric stance against nature that reflects our limited understanding of the universe, we have begun to see ourselves as one species intertwined among others in a brilliantly complex ecosystem of interdependen-cies. To know that the world beyond us—and perhaps within us—is more complicated than we can think is also to imagine—indeed, to submit to—a future in which humans are no longer at the center of things. At the same time, it opens up in the human center a meeting place for all things great and small.

Jeff Kelley (Art critic and visiting lecturer at the University of California, Berkeley)   *for Museums*

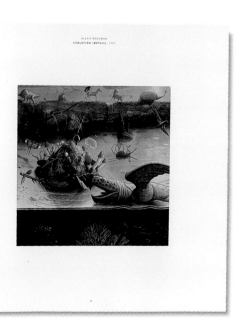

ALEXIS ROCKMAN
EVOLUTION (DETAIL), 1992

MIRES DESIGN *California Center for the Arts Museum*

THE NATIONAL BALLET CENTRE CAPITAL CAMPAIGN

THE NATIONAL BALLET OF CANADA

REID ANDERSON, ARTISTIC DIRECTOR

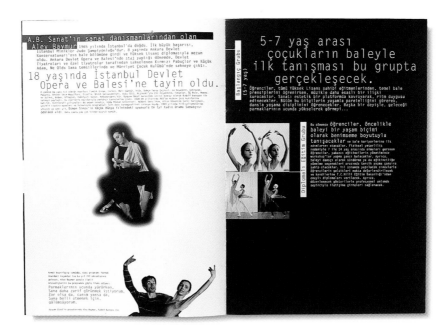

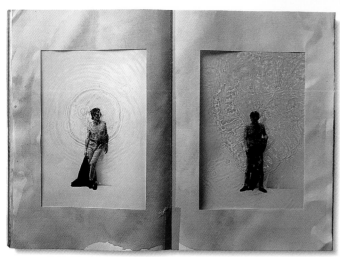

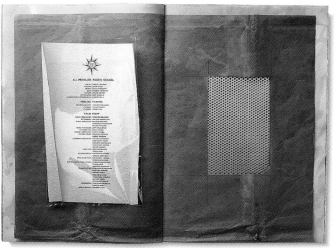

KENZO IZUTANI OFFICE CORPORATION *A.Y.O. Co., Ltd.*

SIBLEY/PETEET DESIGN *Weyerhaeuser Paper Company*

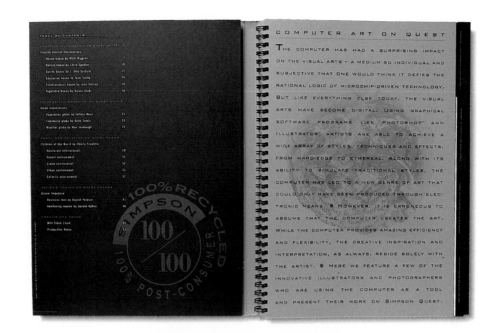

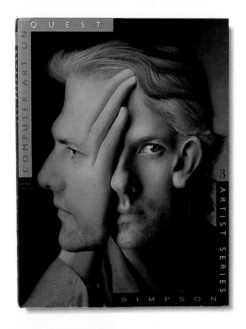

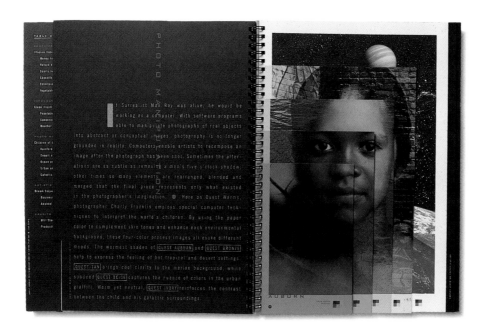

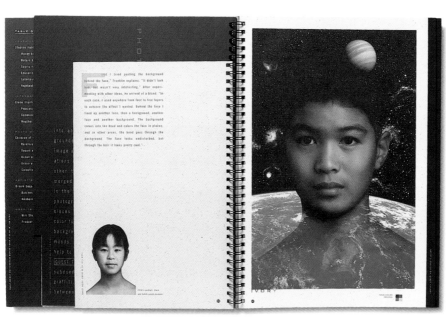

PENTAGRAM DESIGN *SIMPSON PAPER COMPANY*

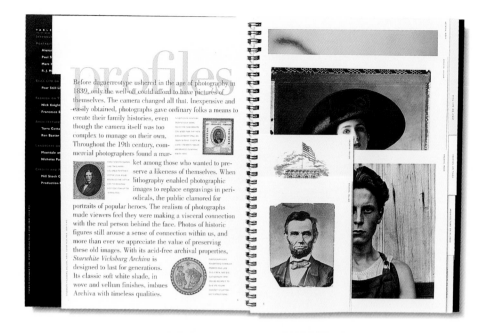

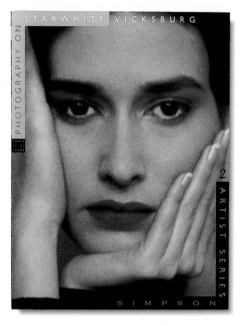

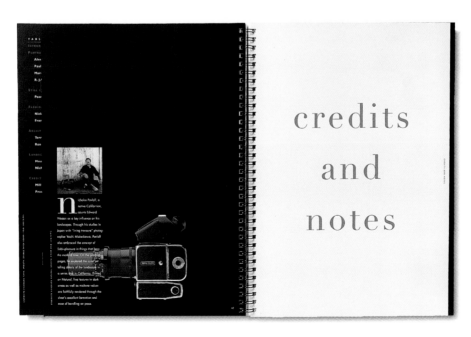

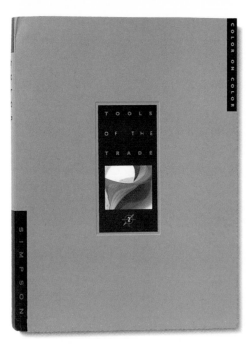

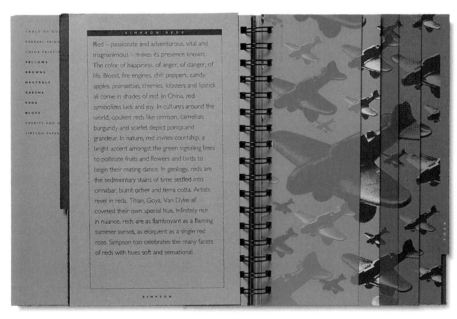

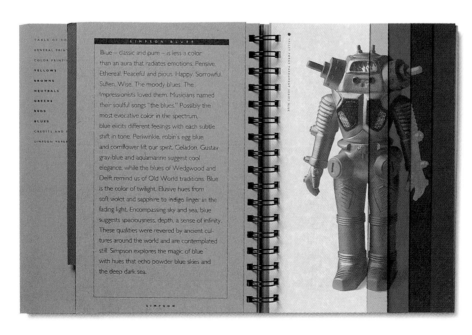

PENTAGRAM DESIGN *SIMPSON PAPER COMPANY*

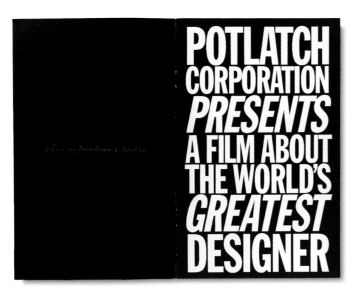

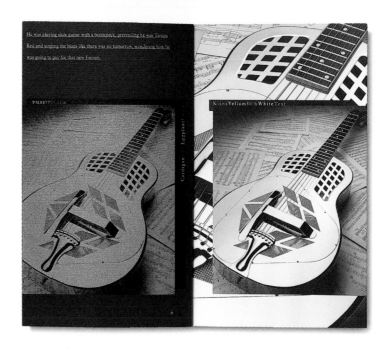

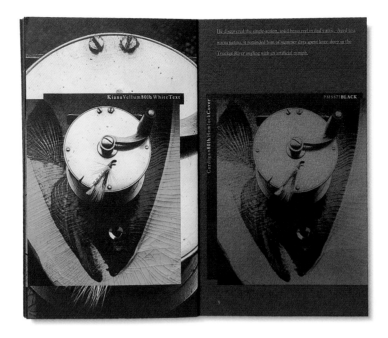

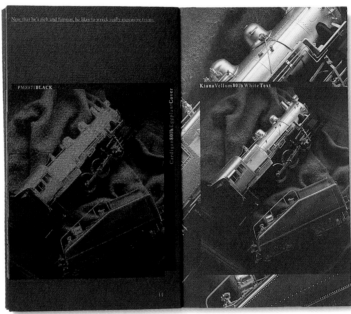

BESSER JOSEPH PARTNERS *HOPPER PAPER*

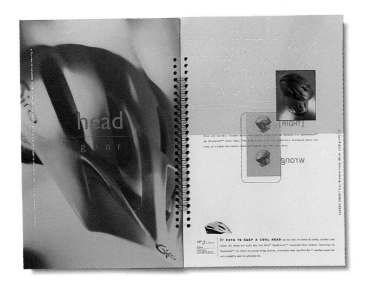

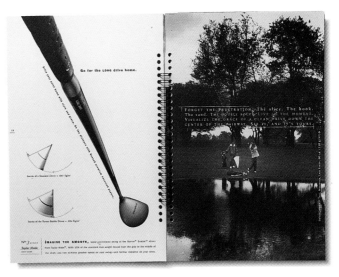

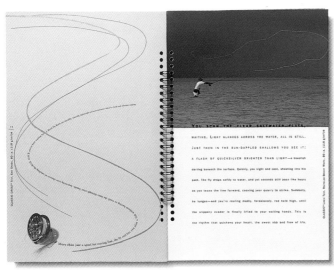

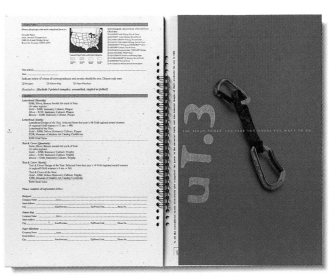

COPELAND HIRTHLER DESIGN + COMMUNICATIONS *Neenah Paper*

Fly the cyberskies!! Forget the stale salted nuts and teeny bottles of English gin. Feed your mind while strapped into your plane seat. Fly Continental and you may find a VDT screen sitting over your tray table. So you can zip around the Internet, fax your office, monitor the NASDAQ and play manic computer games—all while soaring over Nebraska. Better than counting haystacks.

LITTLE & COMPANY *CROSS POINTE PAPER CORPORATION*

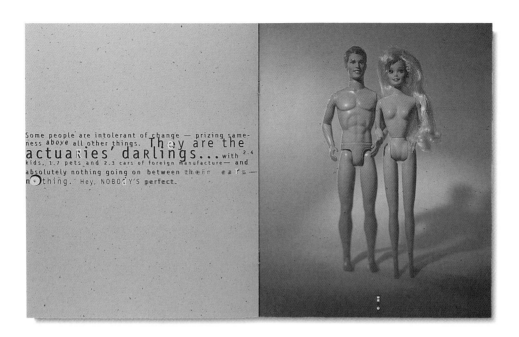

PATTEE DESIGN, INC. *FOX RIVER PAPER COMPANY*

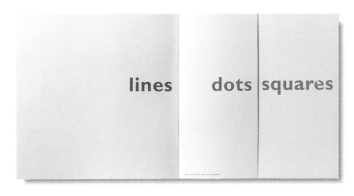

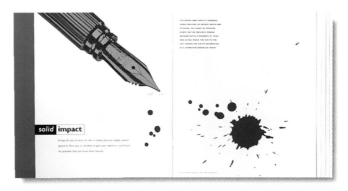

DESIGNFRAME INC. *STRATHMORE PAPERS*

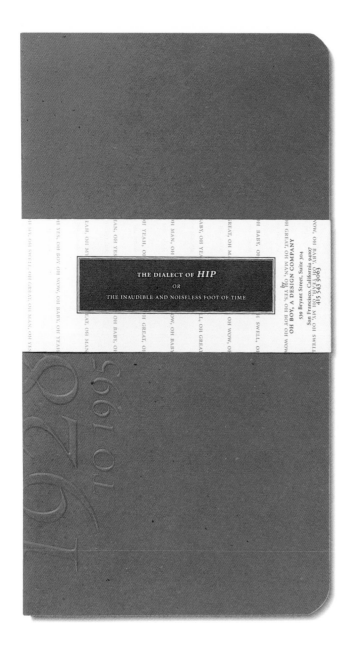

(Left) **OH BOY, A DESIGN COMPANY** *Fox River Paper Company*
(Right) **COPELAND HIRTHLER DESIGN + COMMUNICATIONS** *Neenah Paper*

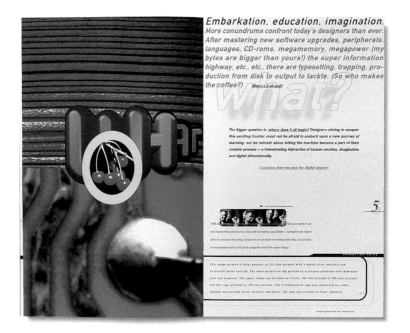

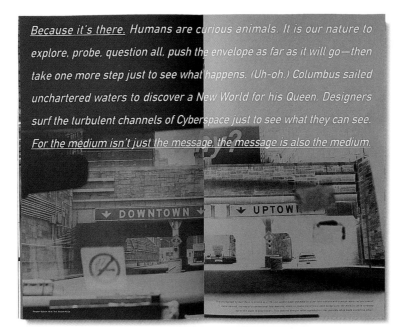

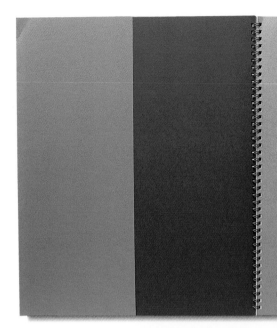

RIVES COLOR offers a UNIQUELY ELEGANT range of paper for CONTEMPORARY printed communications. Use Rives Design or Rives Tradition for their STRONG TEXTURAL CHARACTERISTICS. Combine subtle textures with a palette of modern colours. With 16 distinctive and fashionable shades to choose from, you can be bold, refined, CULTURED and CO-ORDINATED. Eight colours, which are common to both papers, and a wide range of weights and sizes, allows FLEXIBILITY for creative solutions. This brochure, A WORLD OF COLOUR AND TEXTURE, unites paper, process and image through a language of GLOBAL FASHION, culture and symbolism. By using a wide variety of creative printing and finishing techniques, Rives Color's inherent VERSATILITY is shown. For brochures, reports, leaflets, stationery and all your printed material, Rives Color demonstrates that ELUSIVE ELEMENT OF STYLE.

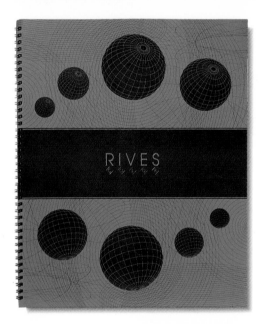

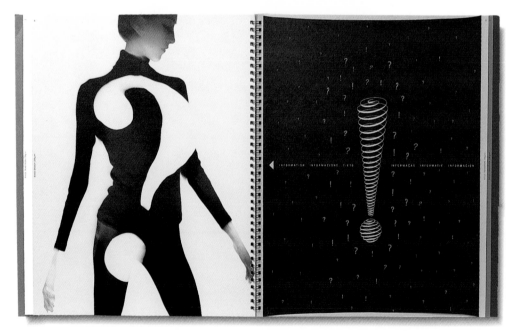

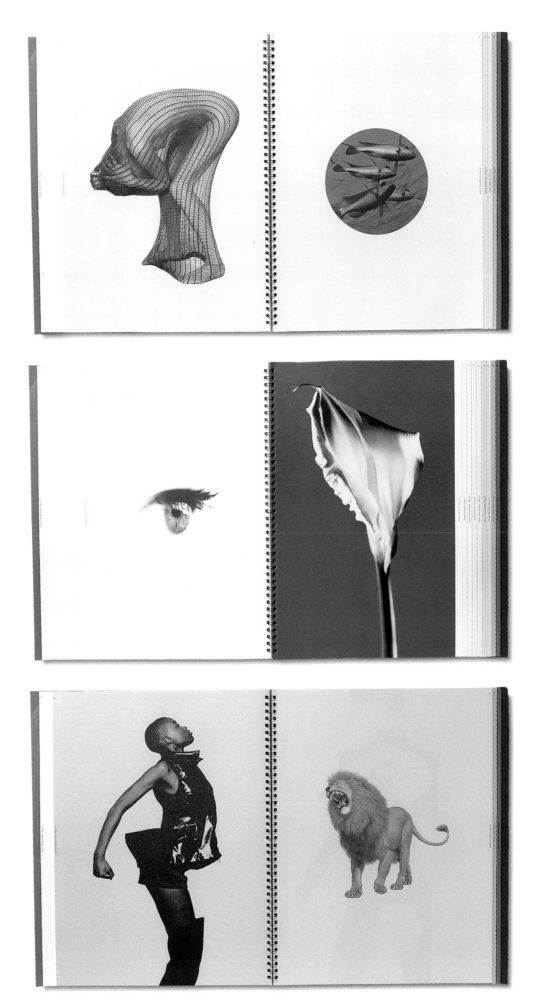

DESIGN IN ACTION *Arjo Wiggins Fine Papers*

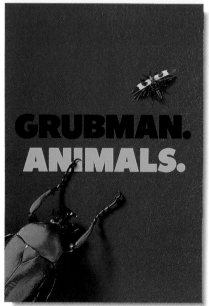

CHICAGO
12,000 SQ FEET

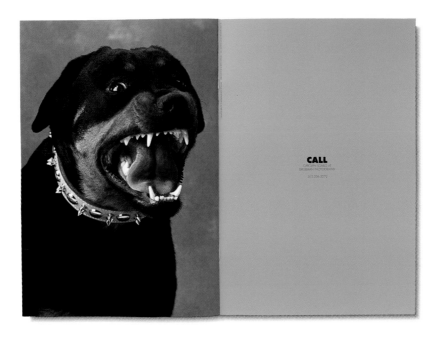

CALL

LISKA & ASSOCIATES *STEVE GRUBMAN PHOTOGRAPHY*

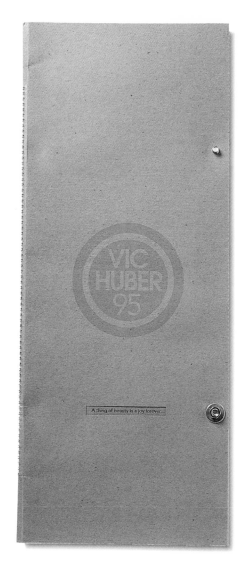

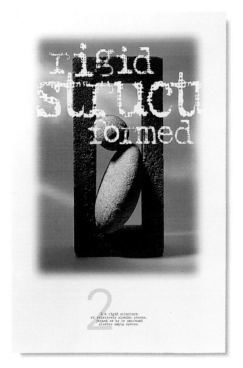

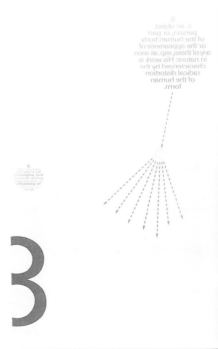

PIERSON HAWKINS INC. ADVERTISING *Brian Mark Photography*

BROADBENT, CHEETHAM, VEAZEY *SHED FILMS*

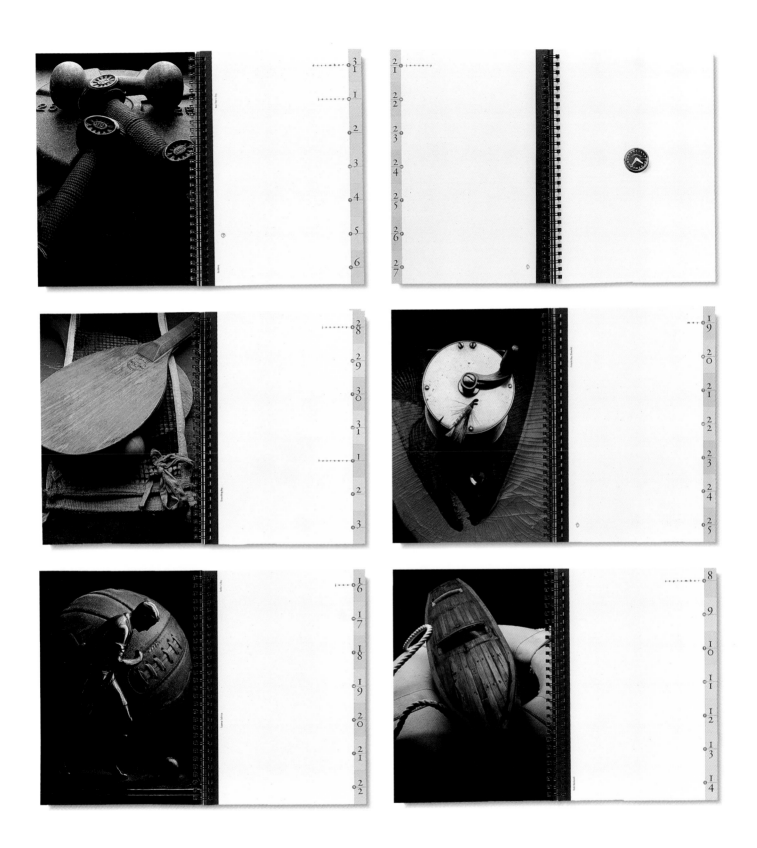

CONRAD JORGENSEN STUDIO *TERRY HEFFERNAN INC.*

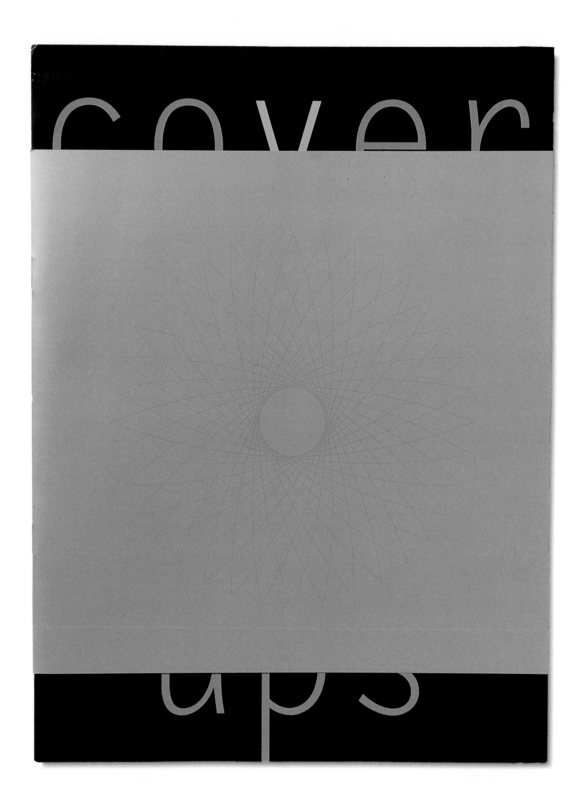

Once again, he glanced in the mirror. What the ——— ? To his disbelief, he saw that the image on page four was a four-color process black and white photograph with spot dull aqueous. The background is a four-color solid with gloss aqueous. The image on page five is a four-color process black and white photograph with spot UV coating on the mirror and dull aqueous throughout.

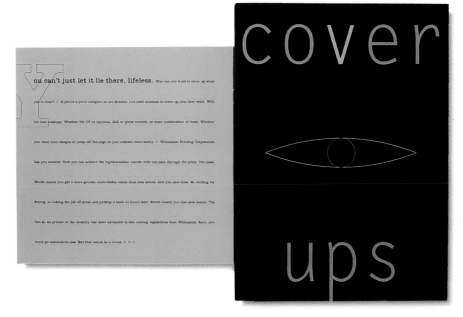

cover ups

Y ou can't just let it lie there, lifeless. Who can you trust to cover up what you've done? If you're a print designer or art director, you need someone to cover up your best work. With the best coatings. Whether it's UV or aqueous, dull or gloss varnish, or some combination of them. Whether you want your images to jump off the page or just interact more subtly. Williamson Printing Corporation has you covered. Now you can achieve the highest-caliber results with one pass through the press. One pass. Which means you get a more precise, controllable result than ever before. And you save time. No waiting for drying, no taking the job off press and putting it back on hours later. Which means you also save money. The fact is, no printer in the country has more advanced in-line coating capabilities than Williamson. Sure, you could go somewhere else. But that would be a crime.

He smirked behind his makeshift disguise. Who would suspect that the photograph on page six was four-color process with spot UV coating on the eye holes, gloss varnish on the car, and dull varnish on the man and newspaper? The photograph on page seven is four-color process with dull varnish on the background and spot UV coating on the car.

SULLIVAN PERKINS *WILLIAMSON PRINTING*

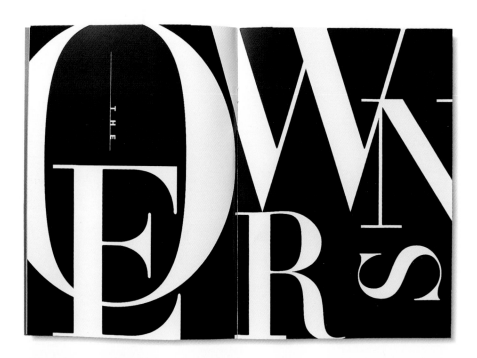

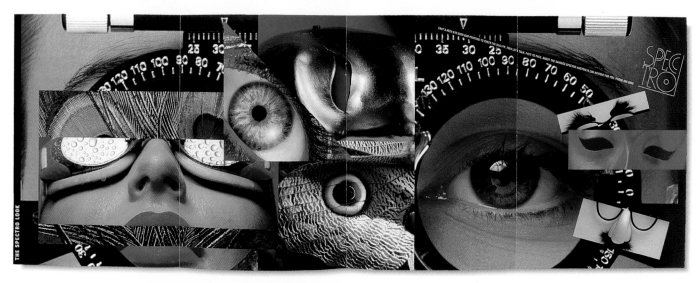

EMERY VINCENT DESIGN *SPECTRO HIGH FIDELITY COLOUR PRINTERS, PTY LTD.*

We registered for
Total Quality Management
accreditation from Day One...
...that's the commitment.

The aim of Total Quality Management is customer satisfaction. With the advantage of beginning with all new equipment, we've organised our plant and processes to meet the requirements of clients. The ultimate is quality control, through the application of advanced technologies, is maintained through every phase of every job. Other quality initiatives include air-conditioning of the entire plant, which provides a stable environment for the machinery and paper stocks, minimising problems with moisture and static. It also creates a pleasant working environment, conducive to productivity and greater attention to detail.

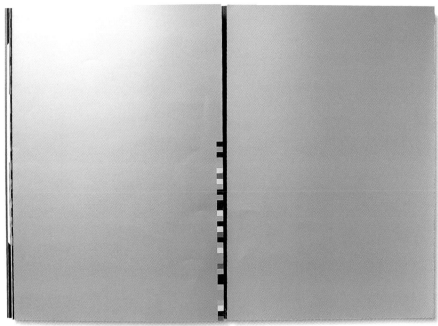

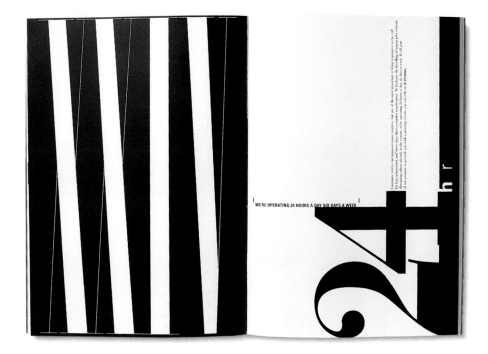

WE'RE OPERATING 24 HOURS A DAY SIX DAYS A WEEK

Customer service encompasses many matters, but one of the most important is being responsive to the call for fast turnaround, and these days don't a regular requirement. To facilitate the handling of urgent jobs without disrupting others already in the system, we're operating 24 hours a day, six days a week. It's all part of our promise to provide you with a printing service you can rely on. **24 hrs.**

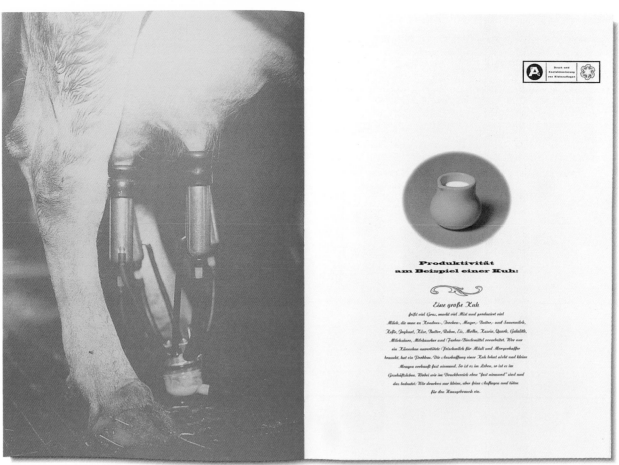

JOERG BAUER DESIGN *FILDERANDRUCK STUDIO*

CUMMINGS & GOOD *CHATHAM PRINTING COMPANY, INC.*

FHA DESIGN *Gunn and Taylor*

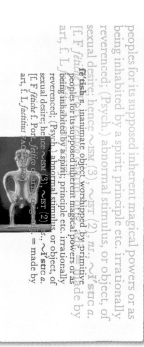

peoples for its supposed inherent magical powers or as being inhabited by a spirit, principle etc. irrationally reverenced; (Psych.) abnormal stimulus, or object, of sexual desire; hence ~ISM (3). ~IST (2). n., ~ISTIC a. [f. F *fétiche* r., inanimate object worshipped by primitive [f. F *fétiche* f. Por. *feitiço* charm, sorcery, = made by art, f. L. *factitius* ~ peoples for its supposed inherent magical powers or as being inhabited by a spirit, principle etc. irrationally reverenced; (Psych.) abnormal stimulus, or object, of sexual desire; hence ~ISM (3). ~IST (2). n., ~ISTIC a. [f. F *fétiche* f. Por. *feitiço* charm, sorcery, = made by art, f. L. *factitius* ~

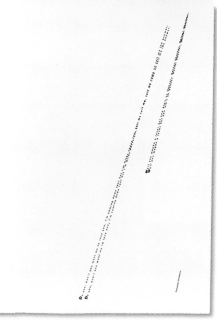

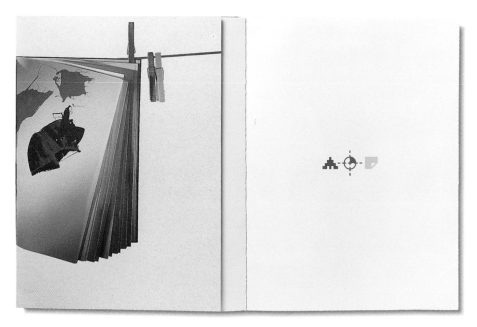

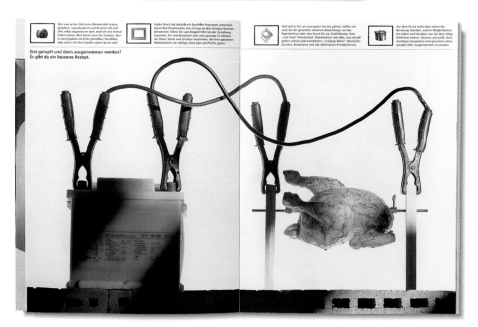

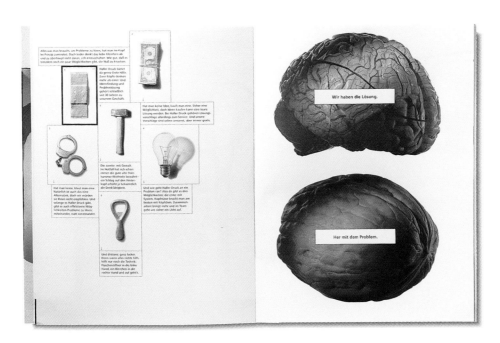

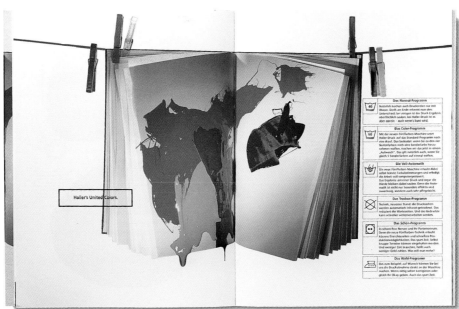

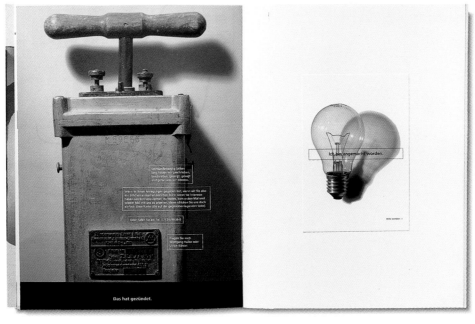

JÄGER & WAIBEL WERBEAGENTUR GMBH *HALLER DRUCK GMBH*

PHILIPPE SAGLIO *LAGUIOLE*

(Né à Laguiole. En Aveyron.)

prénom du roi mage Melchior. Et merci aux autres Mas, Joseph, Jean et Jean-Pierre, les fils de Pierre, le taupier. Merci à Guillaume Moisset qui a laissé le buron de son père pour forger l'acier et à Pierre Raffy, le fils de Joseph, l'instituteur. Merci à Auguste Valmy, venu de Saint-Geniez d'Olt, à Joseph Pagès et à Berthe, sa veuve et à tous ses ouvriers, les Rigal, les Cure, les Benel, les Seguis. Merci à eux parce que ce sont eux, tous ensemble qui ont fait le Laguiole à Laguiole et qui ont donné son âme à ce couteau-là ! ████

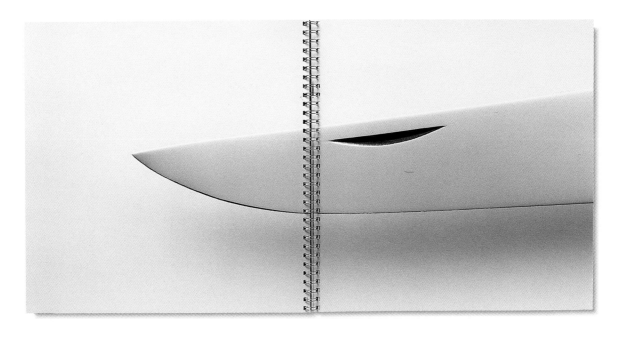

■ls ne roulaient pas sur l'or, les gars de l'Aubrac, au siècle dernier... alors quand le Général Hiver les mettait sur la paille, ils ne restaient pas là, à se tourner les pouces. Ils partaient en bandes vers la frontière d'en bas, celle de l'Espagne avec dans la tête l'idée de se faire embaucher comme scieurs de long ou comme travailleurs d'occasion. Ce n'était pas la porte à côté, la Castille et pour se défendre contre ceux qui en auraient voulu à leur bourse qu'ils avaient pourtant bien vide, ils mettaient dans leur poche le poignard de chez eux, celui que forgeaient les forgerons de Laguiole et qu'ils appelaient capuchadou. De l'autre côté des Pyrénées, on lui trouvait l'air un peu simplet, à ce poignard-là. C'est vrai qu'à côté des navajas qui s'ouvraient et se fermaient

PETITE ET GRANDE HISTOIRE

"... QUAND LE GÉNÉRAL HIVER LES METTAIT SUR LA PAILLE, ILS NE RESTAIENT PAS LÀ, À SE TOURNER LES POUCES..."

pour un si ou pour un no, sa lame qui restait droite au garde-à-vous faisait un peu rustique. Alors, un printemps qu'il revenait au pays, un des gars de Laguiole qui trouvait qu'il y avait plus d'idées dans deux têtes que dans une, dit à un forgeron de chez lui que ce serait bien d'essayer de lui donner un peu d'intelligence, à ce capuchadou-là. En ce temps-là, les forgerons étaient un peu sorciers. Le feu, le fer et l'eau leur mettaient la magie aux doigts. Couteau, c'est masculin mais lame, c'est féminin et l'esprit de la forge qui s'y connaissait en grammaire et en femmes donna à la lame puis au manche

"... CELUI QUE FORGEAIENT LES FORGERONS DE LAGUIOLE ET QU'ILS APPELAIENT CAPUCHADOU..."

du couteau la forme d'une caresse. L'acier le plus dur trempé dans l'eau la plus pure, celle de la source du ●●●

17

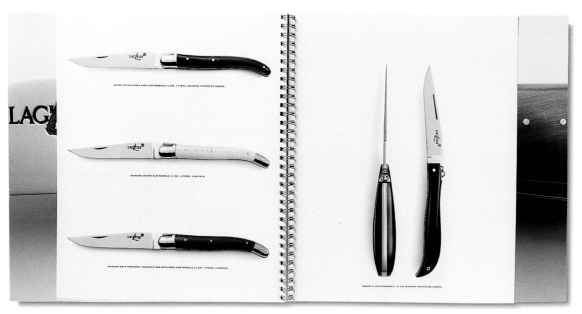

Si les mouches étaient des abeilles, ça se saurait quand même ! Personne n'aurait inventé le papier tue-mouches, celui qui pendait en rouleau jaunâtre au plafond des cuisines pas plus que le gobe-mouches, prison de verre posée sur les tables de nuit. Il y aurait même du miel de mouche, c'est tout dire ! Ecoutez si vous voulez les mouches du coche qui vous disent qu'au sommet du ressort du Laguiole, on peut voir l'abeille qui survola l'Empereur du Pont d'Arcole à Waterloo. Mais si vous passez par l'Aubrac, approchez-vous donc d'un troupeau de nos grands bœufs d'Aubrac. N'ayez pas peur quand ils vous regarderont droit dans les yeux, faites la même chose et profitez-en pour voir un peu partout autour d'eux une autre joyeuse bande en promenade, une bande de mouches de l'Aubrac, jolies comme tout et pas farouches. Abeille ou mouche sur le Laguiole ? En tous cas, il n'y a pas de quoi la prendre, la mouche !

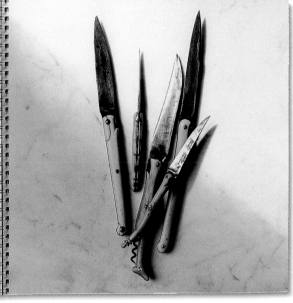

La seule chose qu'un Laguiole ne coupera jamais, c'est l'amitié. Une (MÊME PETITE) pièce de monnaie et le cadeau devient échange et tout s'arrange !

PHILIPPE SAGLIO *LAGUIOLE*

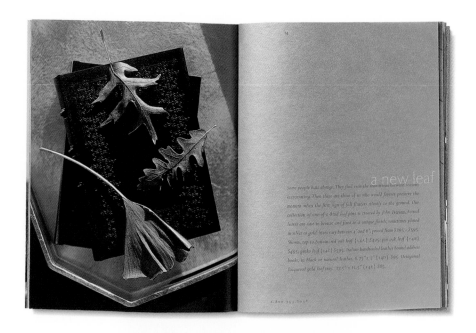

a new leaf

Some people hate change. They find even the transition between seasons excruciating. Then there are those of us who would forever preserve the moment when the first sign of fall flutters slowly to the ground. Our collection of one-of-a-kind leaf pins is created by John Iversen. Actual leaves are cast in bronze and fired in a unique finish, sometimes plated in silver or gold. Sizes vary between 4" and 6", priced from $295 - $595. Shown, top to bottom: red oak leaf {14A} $495; pin oak leaf {14B} $495; ginko leaf {14C} $595. Italian handtooled leather bound address books, in black or natural leather, 6.75" x 5" {14D} $95. Octagonal lacquered gold leaf tray, 17.5" x 11.5" {14E} $85.

1-800-753-2038

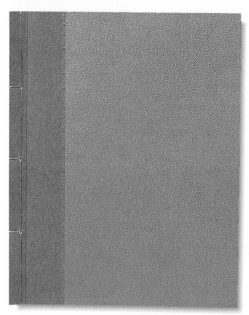

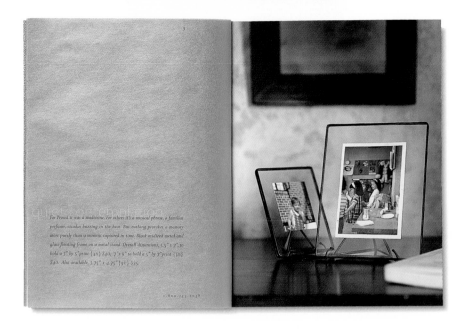

For Proust it was a madeleine. For others it's a musical phrase, a familiar perfume, cicadas buzzing in the heat. But nothing provokes a memory more purely than a moment captured in time. Black oxidized metal and glass floating frame on a metal stand. Overall dimensions, 5.5" x 7", to hold a 3" by 5" print {3A} $40; 7" x 9" to hold a 5" by 7" print {3B} $45. Also available, 3.75" x 4.75" {3C} $35.

1-800-753-2038

Women are so different but. Over coffee, around a quilt or a conference table, in a park or a sauna, they can find common ground. There are certain things that every woman wants. Don't look to Freud for the answer. Traditional Japanese-style suede platform thongs with cotton velvet strap, made in France. Wear them indoors and out. Available in purple with brown, olive with black, green with blue, orange with burgundy; or burgundy with grey. Sizes 36(6), 38(8), 40(9). [17A] $125.

It's all in the presentation. The wisdom of this maxim has never been more apparent. Mundane morsels are rendered sublime by the sheer artistry that surrounds them. Black lacquer bento box with removable dividers, two 4" ceramic dishes, 2.5" square cedarblock, and 4.25" square woven bamboo plate. 10.25" x 10.25" [4A] $35. Black lacquer chopsticks. 9" [4B] $5.

The world worships rice. It's a kind of blank slate upon which every culture makes its mark. From risotto to paella to pudding, spiced with cardamom, flecked with seaweed, studded with beans; it conjures up a sense of well-being. Ceramic bowl with crackled 24kt gold glaze inside and rich persimmon red outside. Handmade in Paris. 4.75" [19A] $125. Limoges porcelain rice bowl with a 24kt gold glaze hand-applied by a French artisan. 4.75" [19B] $75. Matching porcelain spoon. 5.5" [19C] $35. Hemstitched napkins of fine Italian linen. Available in 29 colors; shown, goldenrod. 20" x 20" [19C] $20.

DESIGN M/W *TAKASHIMAYA NEW YORK*

Designed by
Lella and
Massimo Vignelli:
"The Halo"
A Swiss Watch
made by
Pierre Junod

*Our basic concept was
to transform the watch
into a transparent,
weightless object.
To achieve this effect,
we designed a frame
that covers the case
and expands
the glass of the face
into a subtly colored
interchangeable
"halo."*

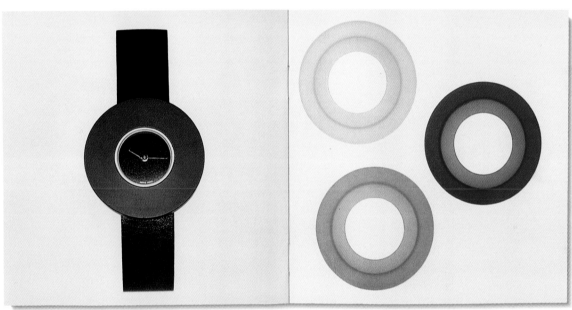

*In product design, form and function are totally integrated;
one does not follow the other. All materials have a special nature;
some are malleable, such as glass or steel, and some are not,
such as marble. With some materials, such as plastics, one can
obtain precise details; with others, such as china and porcelain,
one cannot. All materials, however, reflect or absorb light
according to their surface finish. Light is the master of form.
It shapes the contours of an object, and distinguishes hard from
soft, and transparent from opaque.
In designing products for everyday use, we sense the importance
of a user's perception and we articulate the products to achieve
deliberate connotations— since whatever is perceived is retained
and analyzed in one way or another.*

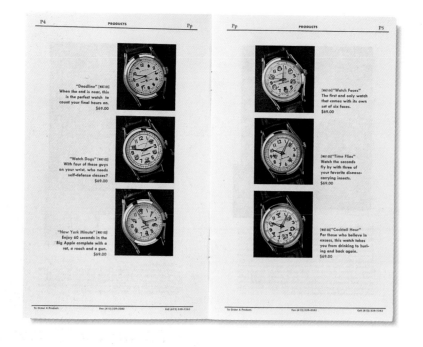

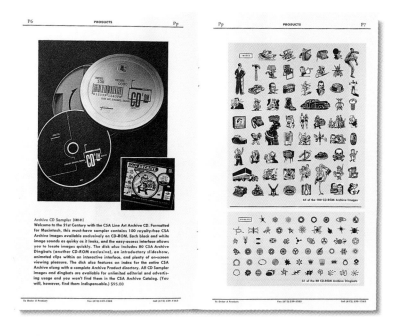

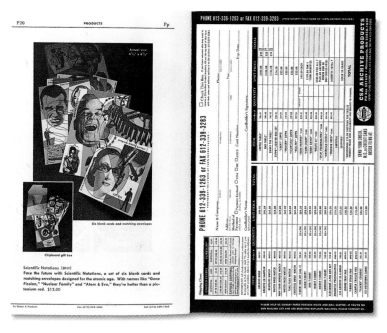

CHARLES S. ANDERSON DESIGN COMPANY *CSA ARCHIVE*

SANDSTROM DESIGN/ARTSY-FARTSY PRODUCTIONS *SOLOFLEX, INC.*

AMERICA NEEDS A *NEW* HEALTH
CARE PROGRAM. MAY WE *SUGGEST* THE
SOLOFLEX® MUSCLE MACHINE™?

THE HEALTH of the average American adult is getting worse. Because of diet and inactivity, American adults will lose over a billion pounds of muscle in the next ten years, and replace them with over three billion pounds of fat.

IT'S NOT A GOOD TRADE-OFF.
Lost muscle means fragile bones, weak ligaments, poor balance, a smaller heart, a rise in blood pressure, a weakened immune system, greater anxiety – all the things we accept as the ills of aging.

YET THEY ARE ALL PREVENTABLE WITH WEIGHTLIFTING.
If you look at the top Magnetic Resonance Imaging (MRI) scan you will see the amount of muscle, bone and healthy tissue on the legs of a 52-year-old man who lifts weights. The second shows you the legs of a 60-year-old man who never lifts weights.

WEIGHTLIFTING CAN TURN BACK THE CLOCK.
Everyone can rebuild lost muscle, with far less effort than you might imagine. The important thing is to start a program now. One that doesn't take a lot of time but gives you great benefits. One that you can do in your own home whenever you like. One that's both easy to start and easy to stay with. You need a Soloflex® Muscle Machine™

SOLOFLEX® WORKS BEST WITH
HEAVY WEIGHTS.

FOR SOME, weightlifting is just not weightlifting without iron plates attached to the bar.
So the Soloflex® Muscle Machine™ makes it easier and safer to use your iron plates at home. Just slip them on the bar and it's like weightlifting with a built-in spotter. Or try a mixture of plates and our Soloflex® Weightstraps." They deliver as much muscle growth as iron plates, but are much easier to handle.

SOLOFLEX® WORKS BEST WITH
LIGHT WEIGHTS.

MANY PEOPLE will want to use their Soloflex® Muscle Machine™ with a light load so they can do more repetitions. This is perfect, of course, if you want to build strength, flexibility and stamina instead of sheer muscle mass. And because it makes the exercises easier to do, you'll want to do them more often.
The important thing is to just do something.

TRY THIS SIMPLE
EXERCISE: PICK UP THE PHONE AND
ORDER A SOLOFLEX® NOW.

SO WHAT'S stopping you?
IS IT THE MONEY? You can own a Soloflex® Muscle Machine™ for just $1195 or $39 a month. With a day in intensive care running at about $2000, it won't take long to recoup your investment.
IS IT THE TIME? Every press, every lift, every stroke is not only pushing weights, it's pushing back the clock. So every workout is adding time to your life, not taking it away.
IS IT THE PAIN? Weightlifting on a Soloflex® Muscle Machine™ doesn't have to be painful. Just start with light loads and increase the weight gradually.
IS IT YOUR LAZINESS? Habits can be changed. But you need to make it easy on yourself. And there's no easier way to get into the habit of weightlifting than by having a Soloflex® Muscle Machine™ right in your home.
IS IT BECAUSE YOU DON'T KNOW THE NUMBER TO CALL? Just dial 1-800-547-8802 now, and your Soloflex® Muscle Machine™ will be on its way to you today.
You'll be stronger, healthier and happier for it. What are you waiting for?

TO ORDER, JUST DIAL 1-800-547-8802

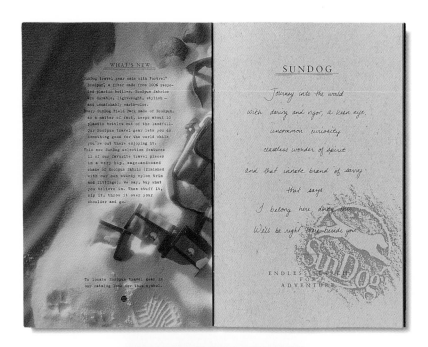

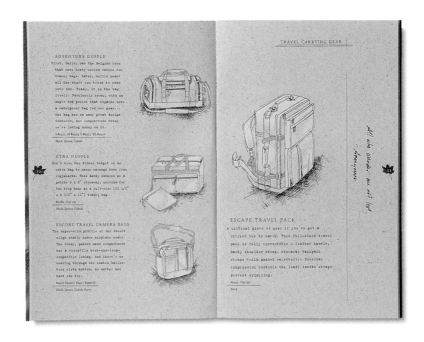

ADVENTURE DUFFLE

First, Duffel was the Belgian town that wove heavy woolen fabric for travel bags. Later, duffle meant all the stuff you tried to cram into one. Today, it is the bag itself. Fabulously roomy, with an ample end pocket that expands into a waterproof bag for wet gear... Our bag has so many great design features, our competitors think we're losing money on it.

XTRA DUFFLE

Don't blow the dinner budget on an extra bag to carry sarongs home from Jogjakarta. This handy stows as a petite 9 x 9" stowaway, unfolds for the trip home as a full-size travel bag.

ESCORT TRAVEL CAMERA BAGS

The super-slim profile of our Escort slips neatly under airplane seats. The roomy, padded main compartment has a versatile hook-and-loop-compatible lining. And there's no wearing through the coated ballistics cloth bottom, no matter how hard you try.

TRAVEL CARRYING GEAR

ESCAPE TRAVEL PACK

A critical piece of gear if you've got a chicken bus to catch. This full-sized travel pack is fully convertible — leather handle, hardy shoulder strap, stowaway backpack straps (with padded waistbelt). External compression controls the load; inside straps prevent wrinkling.

PHOTO

The Rwandan government limits contact time to one hour. Fifty-nine minutes and 59 seconds from initial sighting, to be exact, and their caution is paying off. This endangered band of 22 mountain gorillas, foraging in the dense rainforest of Volcanoes National Park, ignores the click of the camera.

Nature photographer Art Wolfe crouches in the dripping undergrowth and peers down through his lens. Then, a slight push from behind. Art frowns; there is not time to focus twice. But the guide is a distance off. Who...? A mature male mountain gorilla, just under six feet and somewhere over 300 pounds. He has

jogged Art's elbow, with the same casual intimacy you might expect from a stranger in a shopping mall.

Like Art, the SunDog photo gear that bears his name is expert, versatile, and up for anything. Unique hook-and-loop-compatible lining gives absolute configuring control — and makes it easy to rearrange from shoot to shoot. High-density, closed cell EPE foam protects your equipment. Inner cages can be used as shoulder bags or fanny packs. Most importantly, these packs are easy to work out of, and wear comfortably over long distances. Our Art Wolfe photo gear is simply the best available. Anywhere.

MODULAR OUTDOOR COMPONENTS

MODULAR BOTTLE HOLSTERS

We don't mess around with our bottle holsters. They're designed for the quick, one-handed draw. Padded sides hold their shape, staying on the alert to receive. The bottles themselves? They are wide-mouthed, with VERY sturdy screw tops. If you appreciate the finer things in life, you need one — or more — of these.

SHOULDER POCKET

An infinitely versatile space-expander. There are actually two pockets here; the roomy, padded one up front and a tall space behind for sunglasses or maps. Adjustable hook-and-loop fasteners attach easily to most pack shoulder straps.

MIRES DESIGN, INC. *TAYLOR GUITARS*

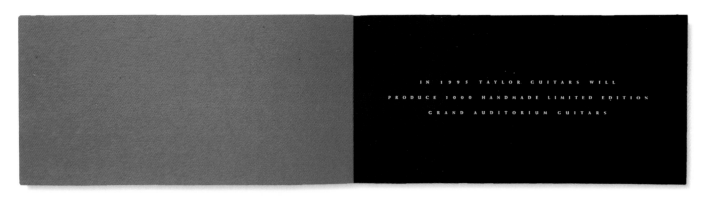

Now, I can get pretty excited about good guitars but generally I get over it in five minutes. But this guitar just *makes* me play it. It just sounds *so good*. A pretty amazing guitar. Over the years I'd heard a few vintage guitars that had a real bright, sparkly bell-like tone that impressed me, and I decided to build a new guitar to produce that sound.

BOB TAYLOR, ON DESIGNING THE GRAND AUDITORIUM GUITAR

1995 LIMITED EDITION SERIES

MODEL GA-MC
TOP Western Red Cedar
BACK/SIDES Tropical Mahogany
BINDING Tortoiseshell
INLAY 1995 GA Pattern
QUANTITY 300

TAYLOR GUITARS

1995 LIMITED EDITION SERIES

MODEL GA-RS
TOP Sitka Spruce
BACK/SIDES Indian Rosewood
BINDING White
INLAY 1995 GA Pattern
QUANTITY 300

TAYLOR GUITARS

IN 1974, TWO YOUNG GUYS WITH A LOVE OF BEAUTIFUL GUITARS AND $10,000 BORROWED FROM FAMILY AND FRIENDS, STARTED TAYLOR GUITARS. TWENTY YEARS OF CAREFUL PLANNING, EXHAUSTIVE TINKERING, LOVING EXPERIMENTATION AND HARD WORK HAVE GUIDED THE COMPANY FROM THAT HUMBLE BEGINNING TO ITS CURRENT STATUS AS ONE OF THE WORLD'S MOST SUCCESSFUL AND HIGHLY REGARDED ACOUSTIC GUITAR MANUFACTURERS. WHAT STARTED AS A PIPE DREAM HAS BECOME A THRIVING BUSINESS WITH MORE THAN 100 EMPLOYEES AND A FACTORY EQUIPPED WITH MODERN, STATE-OF-THE-ART MACHINERY. MORE IMPORTANTLY, THE PEOPLE AT TAYLOR GUITARS TAKE GREAT SATISFACTION IN THE KNOWLEDGE THAT GROWTH HAS NOT COME AT THE EXPENSE OF QUALITY, BUT IN FACT, HAS MADE SUPERIOR RESULTS EVEN MORE ATTAINABLE. TAYLOR GUITARS 1940 GILLESPIE WAY, EL CAJON, CALIFORNIA 92020-1096, USA.

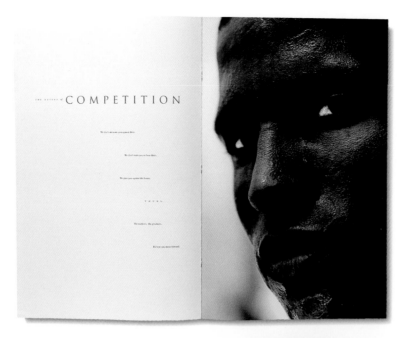

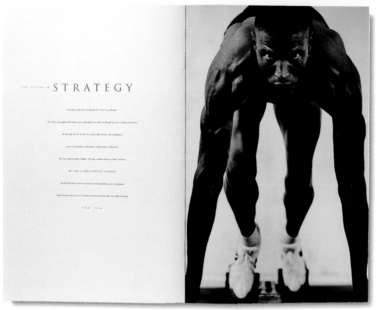

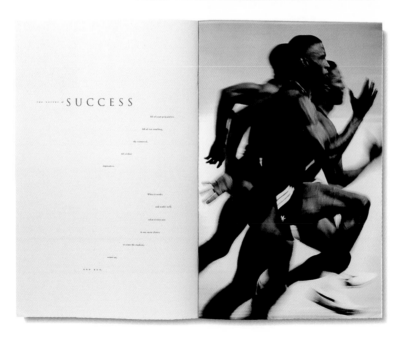

PATRICK MOUNTAIN ADVERTISING *Lai Venuti Lai Advertising*

[JACK MACHOLL]

As a marketer of financial services over the past 14 years, I've worn many hats. I've been a strategic planner, a manager of people, a product developer; I've overseen the creation of new corporate identities, comprehensive marketing/public relations programs and campaigns.

My experience positions me well to be a contributor to the long-term success of a progressive, innovative company.

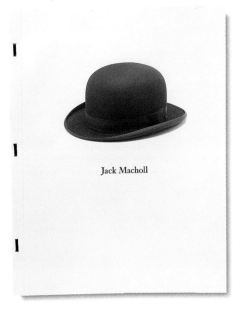

Jack Macholl

[JACK MACHOLL]

I'm looking for a position in which I can contribute to business success – a place to hang my hat long-term.

I'm eager to meet face-to-face to discuss my background and opportunities to make a difference for a dynamic organization.

Thank you for your consideration.

VSA PARTNERS, INC. *JACK MACHOLL*

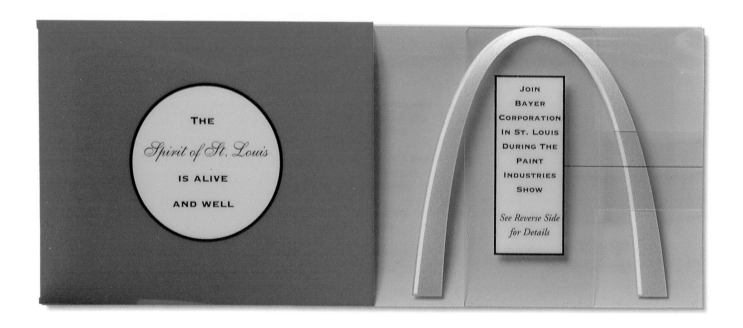

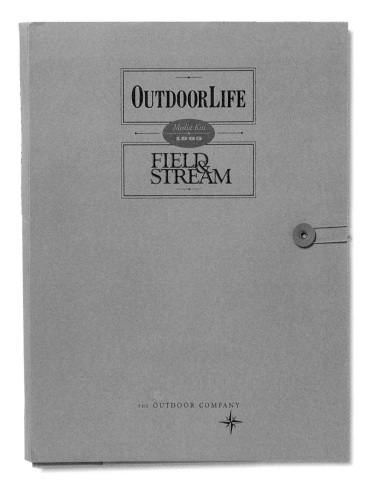

PLATINUM DESIGN INC., NYC *TIMES MIRROR*

Just a month before the end of 1987 came a beginning.
Six people decided to answer the call. And Batey Ads Malaysia was born.

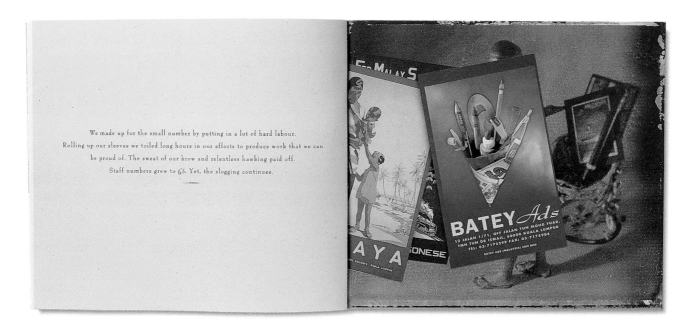

We made up for the small number by putting in a lot of hard labour.
Rolling up our sleeves we toiled long hours in our efforts to produce work that we can
be proud of. The sweat of our brow and relentless hawking paid off.
Staff numbers grew to 65. Yet, the slogging continues.

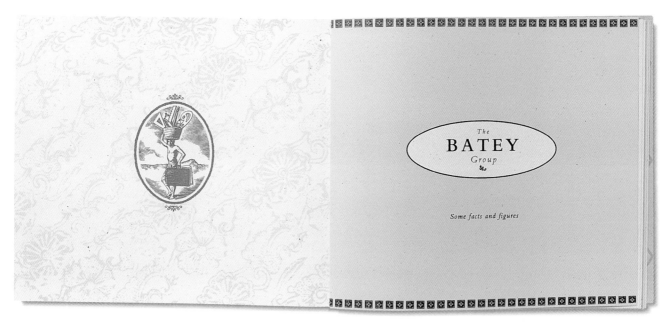

The
BATEY
Group

Some facts and figures

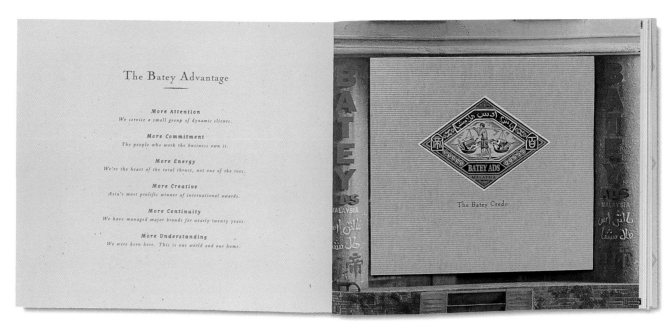

The Batey Advantage

More Attention
We service a small group of dynamic clients.

More Commitment
The people who work the business own it.

More Energy
We're the heart of the total thrust, not one of the toes.

More Creative
Asia's most prolific winner of international awards.

More Continuity
We have managed major brands for nearly twenty years.

More Understanding
We were born here. This is our world and our home.

BATEY ADS SINGAPORE *(IN-HOUSE)*

HEBE WERBUNG & DESIGN *(IN-HOUSE)*

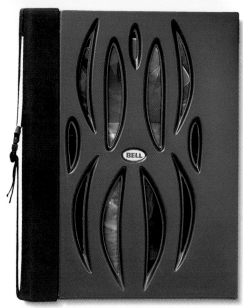

GOODBY SILVERSTEIN & PARTNERS *BELL HELMETS*

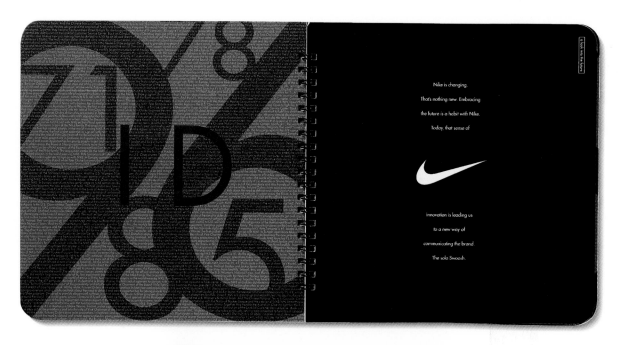

NIKE, INC. *(IN-HOUSE)*

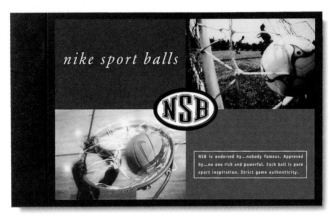

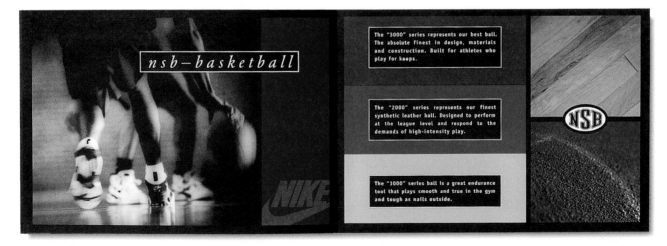

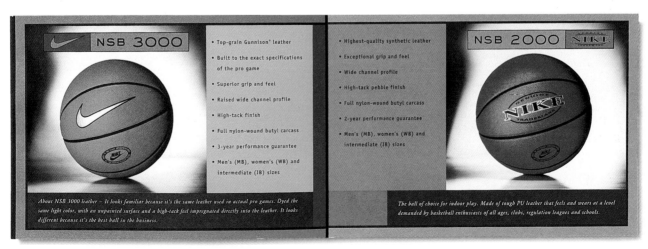

FUNCTIONAL. INNOVATIVE. TECHNOLOGY. WHEN YOU WORKOUT YOU REQUIRE PROTECTION. FROM HEAT, RAIN, SNOW, WIND AND SWEAT. NIKE HAS DEVELOPED TECHNOLOGIES THAT ADDRESS ALL OF THESE CHALLENGES. *NIKE* F.I.T.®

DRI F.I.T. IF YOU WORK OUT, YOU'RE GOING TO SWEAT. BUT ARE YOU STILL GOING TO STAY COMFORTABLE? SWEAT IS GOOD. BUT, TOO MUCH AND YOU'LL OVERHEAT OR GET CHILLED. DRI-F.I.T.® MICROFIBER FABRIC WORKS TO KEEP YOU COMFORTABLE — TRANSPORTING PERSPIRATION FROM YOUR SKIN TO THE OUTSIDE FOR RAPID EVAPORATION. WORKOUT. SWEAT. STAY COMFORTABLE. NOTHING PERFORMS BETTER.

THERMA F.I.T. YOU CAN WEAR ALMOST ANYTHING TO STAY WARM. BUT CAN YOU STILL MOVE? WHEN YOU WORKOUT IN THE COLD YOU NEED TO STAY WARM, BUT YOU STILL WANT FREEDOM OF MOVEMENT. THE TIGHT KNIT OF THERMA-F.I.T.® FLEECE WORKS LIKE A MICRO-FIBER BLANKET — EXTREMELY WARM, LIGHT AND COMFORTABLE. LIGHTWEIGHT FREEDOM FROM THE COLD. NOTHING PERFORMS BETTER.

STORM F.I.T. WHAT'S SO GREAT ABOUT KEEPING WATER OUT WHEN YOU'RE ALREADY SOAKED FROM THE INSIDE? WHEN YOU WORKOUT YOU SWEAT, EVEN IN COLD, WET CONDITIONS. YOU NEED A TOTALLY WATER-PROOF YET HIGHLY BREATHABLE FABRIC. NIKE CREATED STORM-F.I.T.™ FABRIC TO KEEP YOU DRY IN ALL CONDITIONS, INCLUDING RAIN, SLEET, SNOW, AND YOUR OWN PERSPI-RATION. IT WILL KEEP YOU TOTALLY DRY AND INCREDI-BLY COMFORTABLE FROM THE INSIDE OUT . . . NO MATTER THE WEATHER OR ACTIVITY. NOTHING PERFORMS BETTER.

NIKE, INC. *(IN-HOUSE)*

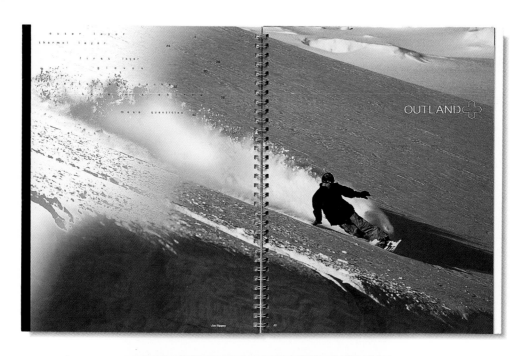

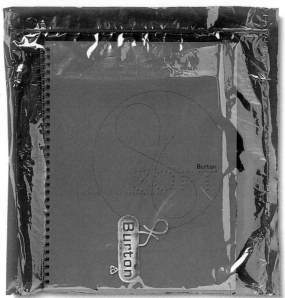

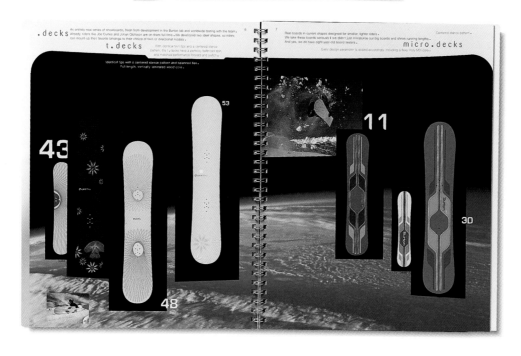

JAGER DI PAOLA KEMP DESIGN *BURTON SNOWBOARDS*

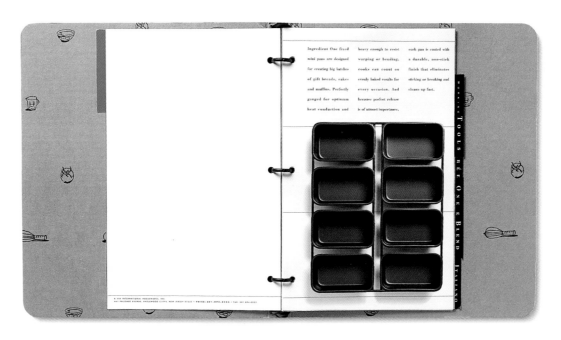

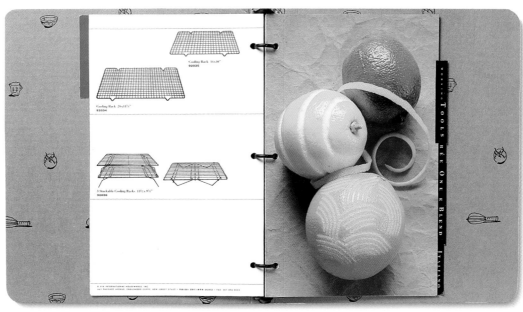

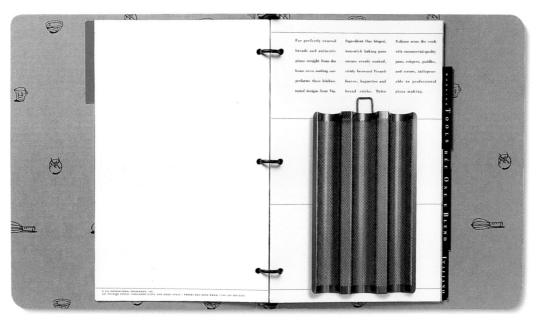

TULINO DESIGN, INC. *B. Via International Housewares, Inc.*

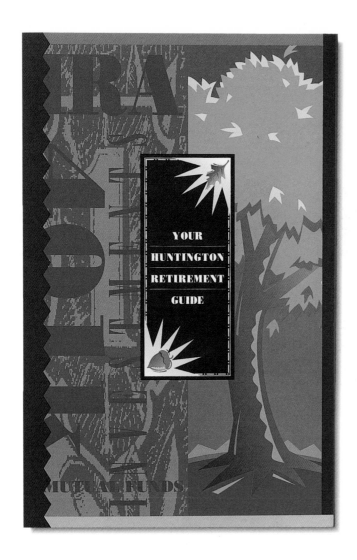

(LEFT) **RICKABAUGH GRAPHICS** *Huntington Banks*
(RIGHT) **JOÃO MACHADO** *Ippar*

ROUNDEL DESIGN GROUP *CZECH TECHNOLOGY PARK*

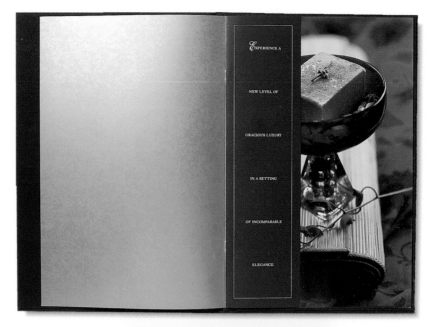

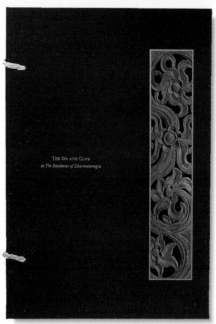

DAVID CARTER DESIGN ASSOCIATES *P.T. Binapuri Lestari*

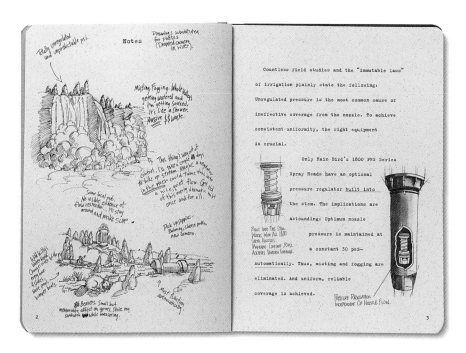

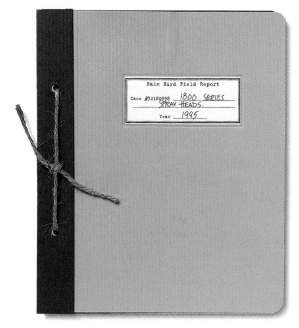

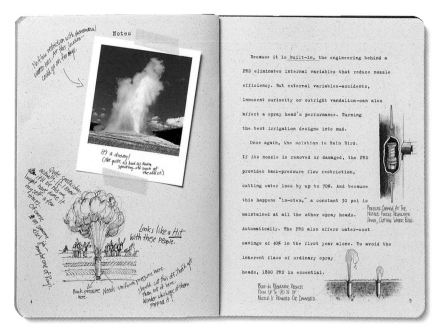

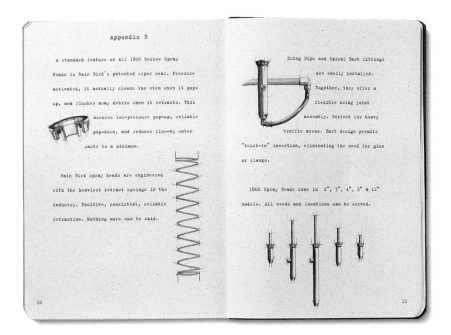

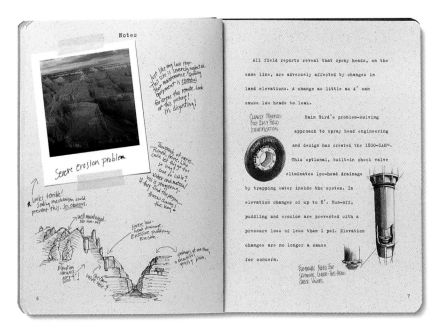

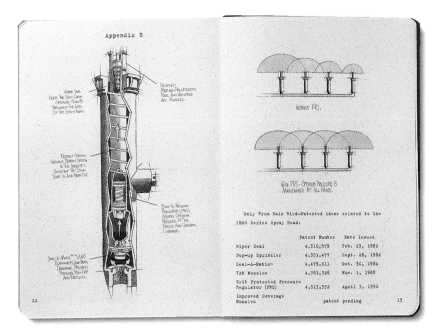

CAPTIONS AND INDICES

LEGENDEN UND KÜNSTLERANGABEN

LÉGENDES ET ARTISTES

PAGE 2 ART DIRECTOR: *Joe Duffy* DESIGNERS: *Neil Powell, Kobe, Dan Olson* AGENCY: *Duffy Design* COPYWRITER: *John Jarvis* COUNTRY: *USA*

PAGE 4 ART DIRECTORS: *Paul Curtin, Keith Andersen* DESIGNERS: *Keith Anderson* AGENCY: *Goodby Siverstein & Partners* PHOTOGRAPHERS: *Various* COPYWRITER: *Eric Osterhaus* CLIENT: *Bell Helmets* COUNTRY: *USA*

PAGE 18 ART DIRECTORS: *D.C. Stipp, Horacio Cobos* DESIGNER: *Horacio Cobos* PHOTOGRAPHER: *Andy Post* COPYWRITER: *Mark Dunn* AGENCY: *RBMM/The Richards Group* CLIENT: *Azrock Industries* COUNTRY: *USA* ■ *This brochure describes tile and pattern combinations that are possible when using the client's vinyl flooring products.* ● *Mit dieser Broschüre informiert ein Hersteller von Kacheln über mögliche Kombinationen verschiedener Qualitäten und Muster.* ▲ *Cette brochure présente les combinaisons possibles de motifs et de carreaux avec l'utilisation des produits du client.*

PAGE 19 CREATIVE DIRECTOR/DESIGNER: *Tim Meraz* ART DIRECTOR: *Debra Girard-Drain* PHOTOGRAPHERS: *Various* COPYWRITERS: *Rich Conklin, Christopher Hoffman* AGENCY: *The Designory, inc.* CLIENT: *Mercedes-Benz of North America, Inc.* COUNTRY: *USA* ■ *This brochure for the 1996 Mercedes-Benz 600 series was distributed in dealer showrooms and as a response piece.* ● *Diese Broschüre über die 600er Reihe von Mercedes-Benz wurde in den Ausstellungsräumen der Händler ausgelegt und an potentielle Kunden verteilt.* ▲ *Cette brochure de produits consacrée aux séries 600 de Mercedes-Benz de l'année 1996 a été distribuée dans les salles d'exposition des concessionnaires et en réponse aux demandes d'informations.*

PAGES 20-21 EXECUTIVE CREATIVE DIRECTOR: *Steve Horman* CREATIVE DIRECTOR: *David Tanimoto* ART DIRECTOR: *Steve Davis* PHOTOGRAPHER: *Various* COPY DIRECTOR: *Rich Conklin* AGENCY: *The Designory, inc.* CLIENT: *Porsche Cars North America, Inc.* COUNTRY: *USA* ■ *This brochure is distributed at dealerships and through direct response to encapsulate the emotive content of the advertising campaign.* ● *Diese Broschüre entspricht ganz der emotionalen Botschaft einer Werbekampagne für Porsche. Sie wurde an Händler und Kunden verteilt.* ▲ *Distribuée chez les concessionnaires automobiles et en réponse aux demandes d'informations, cette brochure se distingue par son fort contenu émotionnel.*

PAGES 22 (TOP LEFT), 23, 25 CREATIVE DIRECTOR: *Tim Meraz* ART DIRECTOR/DESIGNER: *Andrea Schindler* PHOTOGRAPHERS: *Various* COPYWRITER: *Various* AGENCY: *The Designory, inc.* CLIENT: *Mercedes-Benz of North America, Inc.* COUNTRY: *USA* ■ *This brochure for the Mercedes-Benz SL-Class series was distributed in showrooms and as a response piece.* ● *Eine für die Ausstellungsräume der Händler und potentionelle Kunden bestimmte Broschüre über die SL-Klasse von Mercedes-Benz.* ▲ *Cette brochure sur les séries de Mercedes-Benz a été distribuée dans les salles d'exposition des concessionnaires et en réponse aux demandes d'informations.*

PAGES 22 (BOTTOM LEFT), 24 (CENTER) CREATIVE DIRECTOR: *Tim Meraz* ART DIRECTOR: *Debra Girard-Drain* DESIGNER: *Andrea Schindler* PHOTOGRAPHERS: *Various* COPYWRITERS: *Various* AGENCY: *The Designory, inc.* CLIENT: *Mercedes-Benz of North America, Inc.* COUNTRY: *USA* ■ *This Mercedes-Benz S-Class series brochure was distributed in dealer showrooms and as a response piece.* ● *Die S-Klasse von Mercedes-Benz ist Gegenstand dieser Broschüre, die für Ausstellungsräume der Händler und potentielle Kunden bestimmt ist.* ▲ *Cette brochure sur les séries de Mercedes-Benz classe SL a été distribuée dans les salles d'exposition des concessionnaires et en réponse aux demandes d'informations.*

PAGES 22 (BOTTOM RIGHT), 24 (BOTTOM) CREATIVE DIRECTOR: *Tim Meraz* ART DIRECTOR: *Mark Wronski* DESIGNER: *Andrea Schindler* PHOTOGRAPHERS: *Various* AGENCY: *The Designory, inc.* CLIENT: *Mercedes Benz of North America, Inc.* COUNTRY: *USA* ■ *This brochure was distributed in dealership showrooms and as fulfillment pieces.* ● *Eine für Ausstellungsräume und Kundeninformation bestimmte Broschüre von Mercedes-Benz.* ▲ *Cette brochure a été distribuée dans les salles d'exposition des concessionnaires et en réponse aux demandes d'informations.*

PAGES 22 (TOP RIGHT), 24 (TOP) ART DIRECTOR: *Ulrich Lange* CREATIVE DIRECTOR: *Tim Meraz* DESIGNER: *Andrea Schindler* PHOTOGRAPHERS: *Various* COPYWRITERS: *Various* AGENCY: *The Designory, inc.* CLIENT: *Mercedes-Benz of North America, Inc.* COUNTRY: *USA* ■ *This brochure was distributed in dealership showrooms and as fulfillment pieces.* ● *Produktbroschüre von Mercedes-Benz, die für die Ausstellungsräume und potentielle Käufer bestimmt ist.* ▲ *Cette brochure a été distribuée dans les salles d'exposition des concessionnaires et en réponse aux demandes d'informations.*

PAGE 26-27 ART DIRECTOR: *Hans Günter Schmitz* DESIGNERS: *Birgit Geisler, Hans Günter Schmitz* PHOTOGRAPHER: *Peter Sondermann, Archiv für Kunst und Geschichte, Motorpresse international, Pictor international, Ford-Archiv* COPYWRITER: *Peter Sprong* AGENCY: *Hans Günter Schmitz* CLIENT: *Ford-Werke AG* COUNTRIES: *Germany, Great Britain, Spain* ■ *Brochure for Ford on the subject of safety.* ● *Eine Informationsbroschüre von Ford zum Thema Sicherheit.* ▲ *Brochure de Ford consacrée à la sécurité.*

PAGES 28-29 CREATIVE DIRECTOR: *Tom Cordner* DESIGNER: *Scott Bremner* PHOTOGRAPHER: *Various* COPYWRITERS: *Rebecca Rivera, Neil Szigethy* AGENCY: *Team One Advertising* CLIENT: *Lexus* COUNTRY: *USA* ■ *Brochure for 1996 Lexus coupe distributed to dealers and sent in response to requests via phone, mail, and the Lexus Internet site.* ● *Das Lexus-Coupé von 1996 ist Gegenstand dieser für Händler und potentielle Kunden bestimmten Broschüre.* ▲ *Brochure pour le coupé Lexus remise aux concessionnaires et envoyée en réponse aux demandes d'informations faites par téléphone, courrier et sur le site Internet de Lexus.*

PAGES 30-31 CREATIVE DIRECTOR: *David Tanimoto* ART DIRECTORS: *David Tanimoto, Steve Davis, Ron Berry* PHOTOGRAPHERS: *Various* AGENCY: *The Designory, inc.* CLIENT: *Mitsubishi Motor Sales of America, Inc.* COUNTRY: *USA* ■ *These brochures for Mitsubishi convey passion for driving and the technology that substantiates the passion.* ● *Die Freude am Fahren und die Technologie, die dazu verhilft, sind die Themen dieser Broschüre für Mitsubishi.* ▲ *Plaisir de conduire et technologie de pointe sont au cœur de cette brochure.*

PAGES 32-33 ART DIRECTOR: *Peter Winecke* PHOTOGRAPHER: *Jim Erickson* COPYWRITER: *Sheldon Clay* AGENCY: *Carmichael Lynch* CLIENT: *Harley-Davidson Motor Company* COUNTRY: *USA* ■ *This 1996 Harley-Davidson Collector's Edition brochure was created to educate consumers and showcase the new models and the brand in a format which reinforces the image of Harley-Davidson.* ● *In dieser Broschüre werden potentielle Käufer über die neuen Modelle 1996 und die Geschichte der Harley Davidson informiert. Im Mittelpunkt steht das Image der Harley Davidson.* ▲ *Cette brochure sur l'Edition de Collection 1996 des Harley-Davidson a été créée dans le but d'informer les consommateurs et de montrer les nouveaux modèles et la marque dans un format renforçant l'image d'Harley-Davidson.*

PAGE 34 (LEFT) ART DIRECTOR: *Carla Hall* DESIGNERS: *Lisa Mooney, Jim Keller* ILLUSTRATOR: *Jeff Koegel* COPYWRITER: *Rich White* AGENCY: *Carla Hall Design Group* CLIENT: *CS First Boston* COUNTRY: *USA* ■ *This brochure for a private consulting group promotes an asset management program for wealthy individuals. The brochure is used by brokers, investment bankers, and analysts to educate and market to high-net-worth prospects and clients.* ● *In dieser Broschüre einer privaten Beratungsgruppe geht es um Vermögensverwaltung für wohlhabende Privatpersonen. Sie wird von Börsenmaklern, Investment Bankers und Analysten zur Information ihrer hochkarätigen Kundschaft verwendet.* ▲ *Brochure pour un groupe privé d'experts-conseil faisant la promotion d'un programme de gestion de fonds destiné à des personnes fortunées, des courtiers, des banques.*

PAGE 34 (RIGHT) ART DIRECTORS: *Sarah Moriarty, Brad Wines* DESIGNER: *Sarah Moriarty* PHOTOGRAPHERS: *Various* ILLUSTRATORS: *Charles Grant, Sarah Moriarty* COPYWRITERS: *Steve Stafford, Joe Prock* AGENCY: *Rhodes Stafford Wines, Creative* CLIENT: *Texas Instruments* COUNTRY: *USA* ■ *This brochure announced the merger of three divisions of the company into one division.* ● *Hier geht es um die Bekanntmachung der Fusion von drei Abteilungen der Firma.* ▲ *Cette brochure annonce la fusion de trois divisions de l'entreprise en une seule.*

PAGE 35 ART DIRECTOR/DESIGNER: *Marion English* PHOTOGRAPHER: *personal with archival photos* COPYWRITER: *David Williams* AGENCY: *Slaughter-Hanson* CLIENT: *Amsouth Bank* COUNTRY: *USA* ■ *This brochure was designed as one of a series of handmade books dealing with the relationship teams theme. Since the client requested an elegant gift to send to corporate clients, it was important that the pieces be unique.* ● *Eine von mehreren handgemachten Broschüren, in denen es um die Teamarbeit innerhalb einer Bank geht. Da sie an die Kunden der Bank verschickt werden sollte, war es wichtig, dass die Broschüre einzigartig wirkte.* ▲ *Cette brochure fait partie d'une série de publications de style artisanal consacrée à l'esprit d'équipe. Le client désirait un cadeau élégant pour ses propres clients. Aussi, il était important d'avoir des pièces uniques.*

PAGE 36 ART DIRECTOR: *D.C. Stipp* DESIGNERS: *D.C. Stipp, Mat Alancheril, Pamela Chang* PHOTOGRAPHERS: *Various* ILLUSTRATORS: *Various* COPYWRITER: *Todd Mitchell* AGENCY: *RBMM/The Richards Group* CLIENT: *Murata Business Systems* COUNTRY: *USA* ■ *Capabilities brochure for a fax machine manufacturer.* ● *Firmenbroschüre für einen Hersteller von Faxgeräten.* ▲ *Brochure d'entreprise.*

PAGE 37 *Art Director*/DESIGNER: *Jac Coverdale* COPYWRITER: *Jerry Fury* AGENCY: *Clarity Coverdale Fury* CLIENT: *ReliaStar Financial* COUNTRY: *USA* ■ *This brochure for a financial services company was sent to brokers to create awareness of the company's name change.* ● *Bei dieser an Börsenmakler verschickten Broschüre geht es um die Namensänderung einer Anlageberatungsfirma.* ▲ *Cette brochure pour une société de services financiers a été envoyée aux courtiers afin qu'ils prennent conscience du changement de nom de la société.*

PAGE 38-39 ART DIRECTOR/DESIGNER: *Carter Weitz* PHOTOGRAPHER: *Donovan Reese* COPYWRITER: *Rich Bailey* AGENCY: *Bailey Lauerman & Associates, Inc.* CLIENT: *Noddle Development Co.* COUNTRY: *USA* ■ *Corporate brochure for a real estate development company.* ● *Firmenbroschüre für eine Immobilienfirma.* ▲ *Brochure pour un promoteur immobilier.*

PAGE 40 ART DIRECTOR: *Jennifer Kilian Knowles* MARKETING DIRECTOR: *Claire Fisher* COPYWRITERS: *David Smith, Bob Finale* AGENCY: *in-house* CLIENT: *Network Imaging Systems Corporation* COUNTRY: *USA* ■ *"Positive Solutions" is a product brochure for a high-end software developer. The brochure tries to place the core visual and narrative elements of the product in a storybook-like timeline of events through analogies to historical events.* ● *"Positive Solutions" ist der Titel dieser Produktbroschüre für einen Software-Entwickler. Die wichtigsten Aspekte des Produktes sind in eine Erzählung verpackt, deren zeitlicher Ablauf sich an historischen Ereignissen orientiert.* ▲ *«Positive Solutions» est une brochure de produits software. Elle met l'accent sur les principales caractéristiques des produits et les intègre dans une séquence narrative d'événements en établissant des rapprochements avec des événements historiques.*

PAGE 41 ART DIRECTOR: *Stefan Sagmeister* DESIGNER: *Eric Zim* PHOTOGRAPHER: *Tom Schierlitz* COPYWRITER: *Stephan Schertler* AGENCY: *Sagmeister Inc.* CLIENT: *Stephan Schertler* COUNTRIES: *USA, Switzerland* ■ *This brochure was created for a Swiss audio company. The cover incorporates a 'Q-tip.'* ● *Für eine Audio-Firma hergestellte Broschüre.* ▲ *Brochure créée pour une société suisse spécialisée dans les équipements audio.*

PAGE 42 ART DIRECTOR: *Peter Harrison* DESIGNER: *John Klotnia* ILLUSTRATORS: *Various* COPYWRITER: *Roger Morrow* AGENCY: *Pentagram Design* CLIENT: *Hansberger Global Investors* COUNTRY: *USA* ■ *This capabilities brochure was designed for a global investment firm.* ●

Firmenbroschüre einer weltweit tätigen Anlageberatungsfirma. ▲ *Brochure d'une société de conseil en matière de placement.*

PAGE 43 ART DIRECTOR: *Paul Wharton* DESIGNER: *Tom Riddle* PHOTOGRAPHER: *Scott Morgan* ILLUSTRATORS: *Terry Allen, Glen Mitsui* COPYWRITER: *Dick Kuykendall* AGENCY: *Little & Company* CLIENT: *Media Loft* COUNTRY: *USA* ■ *This orporate overview brochure details the multimedia services offered by the client.* ● *Informationsbroschüre über das Angebot einer Multimedia-Firma.* ▲ *Brochure informative sur les services proposés par une société spécialisée dans le multimédia.*

PAGE 44-45 ART DIRECTOR/DESIGNER: *Steve Sandstrom* PHOTOGRAPHER: *Geof Kern* COPYWRITER: *Leslee Dillon* AGENCY: *Sandstrom Design* CLIENT: *Marketing One Incorporated* COUNTRY: *USA* ■ *Informational brochure for a financial service marketing firm.* ● *Informationsbroschüre für eine Marketing-Firma im Bereich der Finanzberatung.* ▲ *Brochure pour une société de marketing de services financiers.*

PAGE 46-47 CREATIVE DIRECTOR: *Hans Günter Schmitz* ART DIRECTOR/DESIGNER: *Annette Ridder* PHOTOGRAPHERS: *Various* COPYWRITERS: *Annette Ridder, Marianne Voos* AGENCY: *Hans Günter Schmitz* CLIENT: *Gira, Giersiepen GmbH & Co. KG* COUNTRY: *Germany* ■ *A brochure for architects and interior designers, in which Gira, a manufacturer of components for electrical installation, presents its switch programs and the advantages of modern electrical installation.* ● *Hauptsächlich für Architekten und Innenarchitekten bestimmte Broschüre, in der Gira seine Schalterprogramme präsentiert und über die Möglichkeiten der modernen Elektroinstallation informiert. Gira ist ein Hersteller von Komponenten für die Elektroinstallation.* ▲ *Brochure pour des architectes et des décorateurs d'intérieur. Gira, fabricant de pièces pour des installations électriques, présente ses programmes de commutateurs et les avantages de l'installation électrique moderne.*

PAGE 48 ART DIRECTORS: *Gregory Beck, Kelly Allman* DESIGNER/PHOTOGRAPHER: *Clarion Business Communications* COPYWRITER: *Gregory Beck* AGENCY: *Clarion Business Communications* CLIENT: *Sony Entertainment Systems* COUNTRY: *USA* ■ *This brochure is a formal introduction to Sony Entertainment Systems and a brief explanation of their products and services.* ● *Mit dieser Broschüre werden die Sony Entertainment Systems vorgestellt, wobei Produkte und Dienstleistungen kurz erklärt werden.* ▲ *Cette brochure présente les systèmes Sony Entertainment et donne une courte explication sur les produits et services proposés.*

PAGE 49 ART DIRECTOR/DESIGNER: *Ulrike Beling* PHOTOGRAPHER: *Jamal Tayeb (portraits), Stephan Schacher (stills)* COPYWRITER/AGENCY/CLIENT: *Hug, von Moos & Dorfmüller* COUNTRY: *Switzerland* ■ *This "Inside/Outside" image brochure and work review for a young design agency showcases the company's work (outside) and what/who's behind the work (inside).* ● *Diese Eigenwerbungsbroschüre einer jungen Designfirma lässt sich von zwei Seiten betrachten, wobei der Leser etwas über das «Inside», d.h. über die Mitarbeiter der Firma erfährt, und über das «Outside», worunter die Arbeiten für verschiedene Kunden zu verstehen sind.* ▲ *Cette brochure «Inside/Outside» présente le travail d'une agence de design à l'extérieur (outside) et son noyau (inside – qu'est-ce qui se cache là derrière).*

PAGES 50-51 ART DIRECTOR: *Michael Sieger* COPYWRITER: *Prof. Christian Thomsen* AGENCY: *Sieger Design Consulting GmbH* CLIENT: *Sieger Design, Architektur + Design* COUNTRY: *Germany* ■ *This self-promotional brochure for a design and architectural company showcases products from 1983-1994.* ● *Selbstdarstellung von Sieger-Design mit den wichtigsten Produkten aus den Jahren 1983-1994.* ▲ *Cette brochure autopromotionnelle pour une société de design et d'architecture montre les produits des années 1993-1994.*

PAGE 52 ART DIRECTORS *Peter Grundy, Tilly Northedge* DESIGNER: *Peter Grundy* ILLUSTRATORS/COPYWRITERS: *Peter Grundy, Tilly Northedge* AGENCY/CLIENT: *Grundy & Northedge* COUNTRY: *United Kingdom* ■ *This brochure was designed to promote the design and illustration of Peter Grundy and Tilly Northedge.* ● *Graphische Gestaltung und Illustration von Peter Grundy und Tilly Northedge, vorgestellt in einer Eigenwerbungsbroschüre.* ▲ *Cette brochure a été conçue dans le but de promouvoir le design et l'illustration de Peter Grundy et Tilly Northedge.*

PAGE 53 ART DIRECTOR: *Michelle Larson* DESIGNER: *Tamra Schumacher-Dorsey* AGENCY: *Larson Design* COUNTRY: *USA* ■ *This "We have a multiple personality disorder" self-promotional brochure was designed to attract new clients.* ● *Diese Eigenwerbungsbroschüre eines Graphikstudios unter dem Motto «Wir haben eine Persönlichkeitsspaltung» wirbt um neue Kunden.* ▲ *Cette brochure autopromotionnelle «Nous avons des troubles psychiques» a été conçue pour attirer de nouveaux clients.*

PAGE 54 ART DIRECTOR: *Gerhard Schuschkleb* DESIGNER: *Brigitte Vegelahn* PHOTOGRAPHER: *Herwig Seemann* COPYWRITERS: *Peter Hauser, Gerhard Märtterer* AGENCY/CLIENT: *Märtterer + Schuschkleb GmbH* COUNTRY: *Germany* ■ *This self-promotional brochure was created for an advertising agency.* ● *Eigenwerbung einer Werbeagentur.* ▲ *Brochure autopromotionnelle d'une agence de publicité.*

PAGE 55 ART DIRECTOR: *Louis Brunelle* DESIGNERS: *Louis Brunelle, Denis Saint-Pierre* PHOTOGRAPHERS: *Various* COPYWRITER: *Alain Benoit* AGENCY/CLIENT: *Parallèle Communication-Design* COUNTRY: *Canada* ■ *This self-promotional design brochure highlights the company's mission and covers its projects in all aspects of visual communication.* ● *In dieser Eigenwerbungsbroschüre werden die Tätigkeit der Design-Firma und ihre Projekte in allen Bereichen der visuellen Kommunikation vorgestellt.* ▲ *Cette brochure autopromotionnelle met au premier plan les activités de la société et ses projets dans tous les domaines de la communication visuelle.*

PAGES 56-57 *Art Director*/DESIGNER: *José Serrano Agency*/CLIENT: *Mires Design* COUNTRY: *USA* ■ *Self-promotional brochure and direct mail piece that showcases packaging projects.* ● *Eigenwerbungsbroschüre und Mailer mit Beispielen der Verpackungsgestaltung der Firma.* ▲ *Brochure autopromotionnelle et publipostage montrant les projets d'emballage.*

PAGES 58-59 ART DIRECTOR: *Torbjörn Lenskog* DESIGNERS: *Torbjörn Lenskog, Anna Svanberg Lenskog* PHOTOGRAPHERS: *Various* COPYWRITERS: *Various* AGENCY: *Torbjörn Lenskog AB* CLIENT: *Beckmans School of Design* COUNTRY: *Sweden* ■ *This brochure for a school of design serves as an information piece for prospective students, politicians, sponsors, and media.* ● *Diese Broschüre für eine Kunstschule dient zur Information von zukünftigen Studenten sowie von Politikern, Sponsoren und Medien.* ▲ *Cette brochure informative sur une école de design s'adresse aux étudiants potentiels, aux politiques, aux sponsors et aux médias.*

PAGES 60-61 ART DIRECTOR: *Anthony Rutka* DESIGNERS: *Anthony Rutka, Priscilla Henderer* PHOTOGRAPHERS/ILLUSTRATORS: *Various* AGENCY: *Rutka Weadock Design* CLIENT: *Hartwick College* COUNTRY: *USA* ■ *Admissions recruitment package for a small, liberal arts college.* ● *Mit dieser Broschüre informiert eine kleines College für Geisteswissenschaften über sein Programm.* ▲ *Programme de recrutement et d'admission pour une petite université de lettres.*

PAGE 62 ART DIRECTOR: *Zempaku Suzuki* DESIGNERS: *Zempaku Suzuki, Masahiro Naito* PHOTOGRAPHERS: *Toshiaki Takeuchi (cover), Takashi Shimomura (interior)* COPYWRITER: *Koji Yamada* AGENCY: *B-BI Studio Inc.* CLIENT: *Hikomizuno College of Jewelry* COUNTRY: *Japan* ■ *This brochure was produced as a guide for a college of jewelry. The brochure describes the college's four-year curriculum as well as post-graduation employment possibilities.* ● *Mit dieser Broschüre informiert eine Schule für Schmuck-Design über ihr vierjähriges Studienprogramm und die Berufsaussichten.* ▲ *Cette brochure sur une école supérieure de bijoutiers/joailliers décrit les programmes de formation de quatre années allant de l'inscription aux débouchés professionnels.*

PAGE 63 ART DIRECTOR: *Michael Cronan* DESIGNERS: *Michael Cronan, Lisa Van Zandt, Anthony Yell, Geordie Stephens, Tripp Badger, Regan Gradet, Lisa Smedley* PHOTOGRAPHERS: *Various* AGENCY: *Cronan Design* CLIENT: *California College of Arts & Crafts* COUNTRY: *USA* ■ *This view book and catalog presents the California College of Arts and Crafts.* ● *Mit diesem Bildband und dem Katalog stellt sich das California College of Arts and Crafts vor.* ▲ *Ce livre de photos et catalogue présentent le California College of Arts and Crafts.*

PAGES 64 ART DIRECTOR: *Kit Hinrichs* DESIGNER: *Anne Culbertson* PHOTOGRAPHERS: *Various* ILLUSTRATORS/COPYWRITERS: *Various* AGENCY: *Pentagram Design* CLIENT: *University of Southern California* COUNTRY: *USA* ■ *This piece was created for prospective students of the University of Southern California.* ● *An zukünftige Studenten gerichtete Informationsbroschüre der University of Southern California.* ▲ *Publication pour les futurs étudiants de l'University of Southern California.*

PAGE 65 ART DIRECTOR/DESIGNER: *Susanne Holthuizen* PHOTOGRAPHER: *Fabrice Bettex* COPYWRITER: *Charmian Norman-Taylor* AGENCY: *Michael Peters Group* CLIENT: *Art Center College of Design (Europe)* COUNTRY: *Switzerland* ■ *This newsletter for a European design school is distributed three times a year to prospective students, sponsors, agencies, design studios, and alumni.* ● *Dieses Informationsblatt des renommierten Art Centers in der Schweiz wird dreimal pro Jahr an mögliche und ehemalige Studenten, Sponsoren, Agenturen und Design-Studios verschickt.* ▲ *Ce bulletin pour une école internationale de design est distribué trois fois par an aux étudiants potentiels, aux sponsors, aux agences, aux studios de design et aux anciens élèves.*

PAGE 66 ART DIRECTOR: *Anthony Rutka* DESIGNER: *Priscilla Henderer* PHOTOGRAPHERS: *David Zickl, Bob Krist, Daniel Husted* ILLUSTRATORS: *Various* AGENCY: *Rutka Weadock Design* CLIENT: *Hartwick College* COUNTRY: *USA* ■ *Admissions recruitment package for a small, liberal arts college.* ● *Mit dieser Broschüre informiert ein kleines College für Geisteswissenschaften über sein Studienprogramm.* ▲ *Recrutement et admissions pour une petite université de lettres.*

PAGE 67 ART DIRECTOR: *Darin Beaman* DESIGNER: *Chris Haaga* DESIGNER: *Susanne Holthuizen* PHOTOGRAPHER: *Steven A. Heller* COPYWRITER: *Julie Suhr* AGENCY: *Design Office-Art Center College of Design* CLIENT: *Art Center College of Design (Europe)* COUNTRY: *Switzerland* ■ *Recruitment brochure for an international design school.* ● *Informationsbroschüre über das Studienprogramm einer internationalen Design-Schule.* ▲ *Brochure de recrutement pour une école de design internationale.*

PAGE 68 ART DIRECTOR: *Bernice A. Thieblot* DESIGNER: *Claude Skelton* PHOTOGRAPHERS: *Various* ILLUSTRATOR: *Ward Schumaker* COPYWRITER: *Linda Thorne* AGENCY: *The North Charles Street Design Organization* CLIENT: *The University of Missouri-Columbia* COUNTRY: *USA* ■ *This brochure was designed to create a distinct image of the university while conveying the information necessary to generate applications from prospective undergraduates.* ● *Bei dieser Broschüre ging es darum, der Universität ein prägnantes Profil zu verleihen und gleichzeitig junge Leute für das Studienprogramm zu interessieren.* ▲ *Cette brochure a été conçue dans le but de donner une image particulière à l'université et d'attirer de nouveaux étudiants.*

PAGE 69 ART DIRECTOR: *Jill Giles* DESIGNERS: *Jill Giles, Barbara Schelling* PHOTOGRAPHERS: *Various* ILLUSTRATOR: *Michelle Wilby Friesenhahn* AGENCY: *Giles Design* CLIENT: *HEB Grocery Company* COUNTRY: *USA* ■ *This brochure for a large grocery company was designed to recruit college students for employment after graduation.* ● *Mit dieser Broschüre versucht ein grosser Lebensmittelkonzern, College-Absolventen als Arbeitskräfte zu gewinnen.* ▲ *Cette brochure a été conçue pour une grande société d'alimentation qui essaie ainsi de recruter des étudiants en fin d'études.*

PAGE 70 ART DIRECTOR: *Michael Bierut* DESIGNERS: *Michael Bierut, Emily Hayes* PHOTOGRAPHERS/COPYWRITERS: *Various* AGENCY: *Pentagram Design* CLIENT: *Brooklyn Academy of Music* COUNTRY: *USA* ■ *This program/brochure was designed for the Brooklyn Academy of Music's Next Wave Festival, an avant garde musical event. Type is partially concealed by the stripes to suggest something "coming over the horizon," a visual metaphor for the festival's focus on emerging talents.* ● *Die Broschüre enthält das Programm eines Avantgarde-Musikfestivals der Musikakademie von Brooklyn. Die teilweise durch Streifen verdeckte Schrift soll andeuten, dass etwas «am Horizont auftaucht», eine visuelle Metapher für das Anliegen des Festivals, junge, aufstrebende Talente zu fördern.* ▲ *Programme pour le prochain festival Wave de l'Académie de Musique de Brooklyn, un spectacle musical d'avant-garde. Les caractères sont en partie cachés par des lignes pour suggérer que quelque chose «pointe à l'horizon», une métaphore visuelle sur le point central du festival portant sur les nouveaux talents.*

PAGE 71 ART DIRECTOR/DESIGNER: *Dan Richards* ILLUSTRATORS: *Dan Richards, Dave Gill* COPYWRITER: *Stanley Hainsworth* AGENCY/CLIENT: *Nike, Inc.* COUNTRY: *USA* ■ *This was an invitation to a media event (held inside a penguin zoo) to introduce Nike's new Storm-F.I.T. fabric.* ● *Einladung zu einem Medien-Anlass in einem Pinguin-Zoo, um einen neuen wetterfesten Stoff von Nike vorzustellen.* ▲ *Invitation à une rencontre des médias organisée dans un zoo afin de lancer le nouveau tissu imperméable de Nike.*

PAGE 72-73 ART DIRECTOR/DESIGNER: *Brian Hawkins* ILLUSTRATOR: *Chris Lensch* AGENCY: *Pierson Hawkins Inc. Advertising* CLIENT: *Denver Advertising Federation* COUNTRY: *USA* ■ *This piece was created for the Denver Advertising Federation's call for entries.* ● *Einladung zum Wettbewerb der Denver Advertising Federation.* ▲ *Appel d'offres de la Denver Advertising Federation.*

PAGE 74-75 ART DIRECTOR: *Michael Vanderbyl* DESIGNERS: *Michael Vanderbyl, Karin Myint* PHOTOGRAPHER: *David Peterson* COPYWRITER: *Penny Benda* AGENCY: *Vanderbyl Design* CLIENT: *Robert Talbott, Inc.* COUNTRY: *USA* ■ *One of a series of brochures to promote products and image for a manufacturer of men's furnishings and neckties.* ● *Eine von mehreren Image-Broschüren mit Produktinformationen für einen Herrenausstatter.* ▲ *Une des séries de brochures pour la promotion de produits et de l'image de marque d'un fabricant de cravates et d'accessoires pour homme.*

PAGE 76-77 CREATIVE DIRECTOR: *Deborah Moses* ART DIRECTOR: *Bridget de Socio* PHOTOGRAPHER: *Ruven Afanador* AGENCY: *Socio X* CLIENT: *Vera Wang* COUNTRY: *USA* ■ *This brochure was created as an in-store giveaway for selected clients.* ● *Diese Broschüre wurde ausgesuchten Kunden im Laden als Geschenk überreicht.* ▲ *Cette brochure a été distribuée sur le lieu de vente en tant que cadeau publicitaire à des clients triés sur le volet.*

PAGE 78-79 ART DIRECTOR: *Zempaku Suzuki* DESIGNERS: *Masahiro Naito, Aritomo Ueno, Naomi Taguchi* PHOTOGRAPHER: *Tamotsu Ikeda* ILLUSTRATOR: *Hikaru Tase* COPYWRITER: *Nob Ogasawara* AGENCY: *B-BI Studio Inc.* CLIENT: *Hideyasu Tase* COUNTRY: *Japan* ■ *This brochure was produced for "Permanent Knit," an exhibition of sweaters knitted over seven years by the late Mrs. Hikaru Tase for her family and friends. Per the wishes of her husband, the brochure was kept deliberately free of any obvious association with Mrs. Tase, while the knitted works were depicted in as dry a manner as possible.* ● *Das Thema dieser Broschüre ist eine Ausstellung von Pullovern, die die verstorbene Mrs. Hikaru Tase für ihre Familie und Freunde gestrickt hat. Auf Wunsch ihres Mannes wurden die Pullover ganz sachlich präsentiert, ohne jeglichen persönlichen Bezug.* ▲ *Cette brochure a été produite pour «Permanent Knit», une exposition de pulls tricotés par Mme Hikaru Tase, décédée aujourd'hui, pour sa famille et ses amis durant approximativement sept ans. Selon les souhaits de son mari, la brochure ne faisait apparaître délibérément aucune association avec Mme Tase, tandis que les tricots sont décrits d'une manière aussi sèche que possible.*

PAGE 80 ART DIRECTORS: *Georgia Christensen, Peggy Bennett* PHOTOGRAPHER: *Geof Kern* COPYWRITER: *Amy Adams* AGENCY: *Neiman Marcus in-house* CLIENT: *Neiman Marcus* COUNTRY: *USA* ■ *This "Art of Fashion" brochure features fashion from various clothing designers.* ● *«Die Kunst der Mode», eine Broschüre des Modehauses Neiman Marcus, in der Modelle verschiedener Mode-Designer gezeigt werden.* ▲ *Cette brochure sur «l'Art de la Mode» présente les créations de différents couturiers.*

PAGE 81 ART DIRECTORS: *Bob Robertson, Georgia Christensen* PHOTOGRAPHER: *Peggy Sirota* COPYWRITER: *Sherri Cook* AGENCY: *Neiman Marcus in-house* CLIENT: *Neiman Marcus* COUNTRY: *USA* ■ *This brochure entitled "Feel Free" features men's fashions.* ● *Dieser Katalog mit dem Titel "Feel free" zeigt Herrenmode.* ▲ *Cette brochure «Feel free» présente des articles de mode pour homme.*

PAGES 82-83 ART DIRECTOR: *Georgia Christensen, Peggy Bennett, Randy Elia* PHOTOGRAPHER: *Geof Kern* COPYWRITER: *Ashley Ferguson* AGENCY: *Neiman Marcus in-house* CLIENT: *Neiman Marcus* COUNTRY: *USA* ■ *This brochure features fashion footwear.* ● *Modische Schuhe sind Gegenstand dieses Katalogs.* ▲ *Cette brochure présente des chaussures mode.*

PAGE 84 ART DIRECTOR: *Neal Zimmermann* DESIGNERS: *Neal Zimmermann, Genes Sotto* PHOTOGRAPHERS: *Daniel DeSouza, David Martinez* COPYWRITERS: *Penny Benda, Neal Zimmermann* AGENCY: *Zimmermann Crowe Design* CLIENT: *Levi Strauss & Co.* COUNTRY: *USA* ■ *This brochure was designed as a guide on how to dress for casual business. Men's fashion is featured on one side, women's fashion on the other. The fly sheets between each page feature notes specifically address sales associates. Also printed without the fly sheets, the brochure acts as a casual dress guide for consumers.* ● *Dieser Modekatalog enthält Ratschläge für passende Kleidung im Berufsleben. Auf der einen Seite wird Herrenmode gezeigt, auf der anderen Damenmode. Zwischen den einzelnen Seiten sind lose Blätter mit Informationen für den Einzelhandel eingelegt. Den Verbrauchern wird der Katalog ohne die eingelegten Blätter als Ratgeber überlassen.* ▲ *Ce catalogue de mode donne des conseils sur la façon de s'habiller dans le milieu professionnel. D'un côté, la mode pour les hommes et, de l'autre, pour les femmes. Les feuilles détachables entre chaque page contiennent des remarques s'adressant tout particulièrement aux vendeurs. Imprimée également sans les feuilles détachables, la brochure sert de guide d'habillement pour les consommateurs.*

PAGE 85 ART DIRECTOR/DESIGNER: *Marion English* PHOTOGRAPHER: *Liz Von Hoene* AGENCY: *Slaughter-Hanson* CLIENT: *Plainclothes* COUNTRY: *USA* ■ *This fall brochure for a retail clothing store is based on the "tailgate party" that has traditionally marked the beginning of fall in the southern United States.* ● *Thema dieses Herbstkatalogs für ein Modegeschäft ist die "Tailgate Party", ein traditionelles Fest, mit dem in den Südstaaten der USA der Herbstanfang gefeiert wird.* ▲ *Cette brochure de la mode d'automne d'un magasin de vêtements a pour thème la «tailgate party» qui marque traditionnellement le début de l'automne dans le sud des Etats-Unis.*

PAGE 86 ART DIRECTOR: *Steve Liska* DESIGNER: *Marcos Chavez* PHOTOGRAPHER: *Mark Havriliak* COPYWRITER: *Jack Sichterman* AGENCY: *Liska and Associates* CLIENT: *American Crew* COUNTRY: *USA* ■ *The client is a men's hair care product line. This brochure is part image tool, part sales tool and is used in salons that carry the products.* ● *Imagebroschüre für einem Hersteller von Haarpflegemitteln für Männer. Sie dient auch als Verkaufshilfe und wird an Salons abgegeben, die diese Linie führen.* ▲ *Ligne de produits de soins capillaires pour homme. Cette brochure sert à promouvoir l'image de marque et est également utilisée dans les salons qui vendent ces produits.*

PAGE 87 CREATIVE DIRECTOR: *Toshio Yamagata* ART DIRECTORS: *Serge Lutens, Aoshi Kudo* DESIGNER: *Takayasu Yamada* PHOTOGRAPHER/COPYWRITER: *Serge Lutens* AGENCY/CLIENT: *Shiseido Company, Ltd.* COUNTRY: *Japan* ■ *This brochure was created in-house for an international cosmetics company.* ● *Diese Broschüre eines der grössten japanischen Kosmetikhersteller wurde im Hause entworfen.* ▲ *Brochure créée pour une société internationale de cosmétiques.*

PAGE 88 CREATIVE DIRECTOR: *Judy Kirpich* ART DIRECTOR: *Melanie Bass Pollard* DESIGNERS: *Melanie Bass Pollard, David Collins, Gregg Glaviano* PHOTOGRAPHER: *Steve Biver (cover), Michael Biondo (fashion)* COPYWRITER: *Jake Pollard* AGENCY: *Grafik Communications, Ltd. (concept/design), Pollard Creative (copy)* CLIENT: *Karla Colletto* COUNTRY: *USA* ■ *This economical brochure was designed to be handbound by the client for customized updates. It serves a dual purpose: to introduce a new swimwear line and to provide a general portfolio.* ● *Diese Broschüre wurde von der Auftraggeberin handgebunden, um eine ständige Aktualisierung zu ermöglichen. Sie diente zur Einführung einer neuen Bademodelinie und als allgemeiner Katalog.* ▲ *Cette brochure a été conçue pour être reliée à la main par le client afin qu'il puisse faire des mises à jour personnalisées. Elle remplit un double objectif: lancer une nouvelle ligne de maillots de bains et servir de catalogue général.*

PAGE 89 ART DIRECTOR/DESIGNER: *Antonie Reinhard* PHOTOGRAPHER: *Serge Guerand, Jürg Bernhardt* COPYWRITER: *Stephan Michel* AGENCY: *Seiler DDB Berne* CLIENT: *Bally Management AG* COUNTRY: *Switzerland* ■ *This brochure presents new collections for each season in a magazine format, featuring fashion and background on locations.* ● *Die neuen Bally-Kollektionen für die verschiedenen Jahreszeiten werden im Magazinformat vorgestellt, wobei nicht nur über die Mode, sondern auch über die Aufnahmeorte informiert wird.* ▲ *Cette brochure présente les nouvelles collections Bally pour chaque saison dans un format magazine. Elle fournit également des informations sur les lieux de prises de vue.*

PAGE 89 ART DIRECTOR/DESIGNER: *Antonie Reinhard* PHOTOGRAPHERS: *Various* COPYWRITER: *Stephan Michel* AGENCY: *Seiler DDB Berne* CLIENT: *Bally Management AG* COUNTRY: *Switzerland* ■ *This brochure presents new collections for each season in a magazine format, featuring fashion, and background on locations.* ● *Die neuen Bally-Kollektionen für die verschiedenen Jahreszeiten werden im Magazinformat vorgestellt, wobei nicht nur über die Mode, sondern auch ausführlich über die Aufnahmeorte informiert wird.* ▲ *Cette brochure présente les nouvelles collections Bally pour chaque saison dans un format magazine. Elle fournit également des informations sur les lieux de prises de vue.*

PAGES 90-91 ART DIRECTOR/DESIGNER: *Antonie Reinhard* PHOTOGRAPHERS: *Various* COPYWRITER: *Christian Jaquet* AGENCY: *Seiler DDB Berne* CLIENT: *Bally Management AG* COUNTRY: *Switzerland* ■ *This corporate identity brochure for Bally was designed to be a motivational instrument for employees.* ● *Diese Image-Broschüre für Bally war als Motivation für das Personal gedacht.* ▲ *Cette brochure sur l'identité institutionnelle de Bally a été conçue dans le but de motiver les membres du personnel.*

PAGE 92 ART DIRECTORS: *Paul Curtin, Keith Anderson* DESIGNER: *Keith Anderson* PHOTOGRAPHERS: *Jim Erickson (environments), James Wojcik (products)* AGENCY: *Goodby, Silverstein & Partners* CLIENT: *Haggar Clothing Co.* COUNTRY: *USA* ■ *This brochure featuring the client's apparel was designed for salespeople to use with their customers to help reposition the company.* ● *Katalog zur Unterstützung des Aussendienstes; es geht dabei um die Neupositionierung der Firma.* ▲ *Catalogue destiné au service externe. Le personnel de vente l'utilise pour ses clients dans le but de repositionner la société.*

PAGE 93 ART DIRECTOR: *Christian Satek* DESIGNER: *Robert La Roche* PHOTOGRAPHERS: *Thomas Popinger (stills), Gerhard Heller (portrait)* COPYWRITER: *Robert La Roche* AGENCY: *Robert La Roche in-house* CLIENT: *Lunettes Robert La Roche* COUNTRY: *Austria* ■ *This brochure/sales folder presents a new aluminum eyewear collection and is mailed to customers, distributors, and* *retailers prior to international trade fairs or before visits by sales associates to optical shops.* ● *Verkaufskatalog für eine neue Brillenkollektion aus Aluminium. Sie wurde vor internationalen Fachmessen an Kunden, Grossverteiler und den Einzelhandel verschickt oder auch an Optikergeschäfte vor dem Besuch der Vertreter.* ▲ *Brochure présentant de nouvelles lunettes en aluminium. Elle a d'abord été envoyée aux clients, aux distributeurs et aux détaillants avant d'être présentée lors de salons internationaux et chez les opticiens.*

PAGES 94-95 ART DIRECTOR: *Michael Bierut* PHOTOGRAPHERS/ILLUSTRATORS/COPYWRITERS: *Various* AGENCY: *Pentagram Design* CLIENT: *Council of Fashion Designers of America* COUNTRY: *USA* ■ *This program was designed for a leading US fashion trade association annual awards gala. It featured the pre-determined winners of various awards and served as a souvenir.* ● *Programm für die jährlich stattfindende Preis-Gala eines führenden Modeverbandes der USA. Es gibt Auskunft über die Gewinner der verschiedenen Preise und dient zudem als Souvenir.* ▲ *Ce programme a été conçu pour le gala annuel d'une des plus grandes associations professionnelles américaines de mode. Le programme de cet événement présente les gagnants d'un concours et sert de souvenir.*

PAGE 96 ART DIRECTOR: *Antero Ferreira* DESIGNERS: *Antero Ferreira, Jorge Serra* PHOTOGRAPHER: *Oscar de Almeida* COPYWRITER: *Luciana Vieira Campos* AGENCY: *Antero Ferreira Design, Lda.* CLIENT: *For Ever Group* COUNTRY: *Portugal* ■ *The purpose of this catalog is to transmit a global view of the footwear components to actual and potential clients. It is printed in four languages.* ● *Dieser Katalog gibt einen Überblick über die verschiedenen Teile, die zur Herstellung von Schuhen notwendig sind. Er wurde in vier Sprachen gedruckt.* ▲ *Le but de ce catalogue était de présenter les différents éléments nécessaires à la fabrication de chaussures. Il a été imprimé en quatre langues.*

PAGE 97 ART DIRECTOR: *Del Terrelonge* DESIGNERS: *Del Terrelonge, Karen Oikonen* PHOTOGRAPHER: *Shin Sugino* COPYWRITER: *Robin Lewis* AGENCY: *Terrelonge* CLIENT: *Elite Model Management Toronto* COUNTRY: *Canada* ■ *This brochure was sent out to announce the amalgamation of three modeling agencies.* ● *Mit dieser Broschüre wird über den Zusammenschluss von drei Modellagenturen informiert.* ▲ *Cette brochure a été envoyée pour annoncer la fusion de trois agences de mannequins.*

PAGES 98-99 ART DIRECTOR/DESIGNER: *Neil Powell* PHOTOGRAPHERS: *Mark La Favor, Hugh Kretschmer* COPYWRITER: *John Jarvis* AGENCY: *Duffy Design* CLIENT: *The Wieland Furniture Company* COUNTRY: *USA* ■ *The client, known for its furniture products targeting the health care industry, wanted to move into the architectural and design arena without disenfranchising its current clients. The objective was to create a capabilities brochure which would infuse the client's manufacturing capabilities with its business philosophy.* ● *Der Auftraggeber, bekannt für seine Möbel für das Gesundheitswesen, wollte in den Bereich Architektur und Design vordringen, ohne seine bisherigen Abnehmer zu verunsichern. Bei der Broschüre ging es um eine Darstellung der Firmentätigkeit, der Herstellungskapazität und der Geschäftspolitik.* ▲ *Le client, connu pour ses meubles destinés au secteur de la santé, voulait se diversifier dans le domaine du design et de l'architecture sans inquiéter pour autant ses clients habituels. L'objectif était de présenter les activités de la société, ses capacités de production et sa philosophie.*

PAGE 100 ART DIRECTOR: *Mauricio Arias* DESIGNERS: *Mauricio Arias, Karin Bryant* ILLUSTRATOR: *Mauricio Arias* COPYWRITER: *Pottery Barn* AGENCY: *Arias Associates* CLIENT: *Pottery Barn* COUNTRY: *USA* ■ *These brochures were created for a retail chain specializing in home furnishings. The brochures give hints to customers who want to create their own home interiors.* ● *Diese Broschüren für eine Einzelhandelskette, die Einrichtungsgegenstände anbietet, ist als Einrichtungsratgeber für den Endverbraucher gedacht.* ▲ *Ces brochures ont été créées pour une chaîne de vente au détail spécialisée dans les articles d'ameublement. Les brochures donnent des conseils aux clients qui veulent créer leur propre intérieur.*

PAGE 101 ART DIRECTOR/DESIGNER/PHOTOGRAPHER: *Chris Solwar* COPYWRITER: *Coco Kim* AGENCY: *Knoll Graphics* CLIENT: *Knoll* COUNTRY: *USA* ■ *The client, a global manufacturer of home and office furniture, wanted to highlight the fact that 30 of its product designs have been included in the design collection of the New York Museum of Modern Art. The brochure showed ten pieces from the studio collection, and was distributed internally and to sales associates worldwide.* ● *Knoll, ein weltweit tätiger Hersteller von Möbeln für Heim und Büro, wollte mit dieser international eingesetzten Broschüre darauf hinweisen, dass 30 Produkte der Firma in die Sammlung des Museums of Modern Art in New York aufgenommen wurden. Gezeigt sind zehn Produkte der Studio Collection.* ▲ *Le client, un fabricant de meubles de bureaux et pour la maison, voulait faire ressortir le fait que 30 de ces modèles font partie de la collection du Musée d'Art Moderne de New York. La brochure montre dix articles de la collection Studio.*

PAGE 102-103 ART DIRECTOR: *Urs Schwerzmann* PHOTOGRAPHER: *Peter M. Vogt* COPYWRITER: *Urs Schwerzmann* AGENCY: *Urs V. Schwerzmann* CLIENT: *Elka GmbH & Co.* COUNTRY: *Germany* ■ *This brochure showcases different programs offered by a German furniture manufacturer.* ● *Hier werden die verschiedenen Programme eines deutschen Möbelherstellers vorgestellt.* ▲ *Cette brochure met l'accent sur différents programmes proposés par un fabricant de meubles allemand.*

PAGE 104 ART DIRECTOR/DESIGNER: *Susan Moriguchi* PHOTOGRAPHER: *Carlo Lavatori* AGENCY: *Susan Moriguchi* CLIENT: *Idee Co., Ltd* COUNTRY: *Japan* ■ *This promotional brochure was designed for a company which manufactures and designs interior objects, furniture, and textiles. The brochure places emphasis on the designers who were commissioned to produce the furniture.* ● *Broschüre für eine Firma, die Einrichtungsgegenstände, Möbel und Textilien herstellt. Das zentrale Thema sind die Designer, die mit der Gestaltung der Möbel beauftragt waren.* ▲ *Cette brochure a été réalisée pour une société qui fabrique des objets design, des meubles et des tissus. Elle met en exergue les designers qui ont été mandatés pour la conception des meubles.*

PAGE 105 ART DIRECTOR: *Pui-Pui Li* DESIGNERS: *Pui-Pui Li, Eric Jones* PHOTOGRAPHER: *Various* ILLUSTRATOR/COPYWRITER: *Eric Jones* AGENCY: *Jones Studio Limited* CLIENT: *M2L* COUNTRY: *USA* ■ *This brochure was produced for an American high-end furniture dealer representing several European lines. The goal was to entice customers with the variety of products available and to communicate the company's philosophy regarding value and service.* ● *Katalog für einen amerikanischen Händler hochwertiger Möbel aus Europa. Das Thema war die Vielfalt des Angebots, der Qualitätsanspruch der Firma und ihr Service.* ▲ *Cette brochure pour un marchand de meubles américain présente plusieurs lignes européennes. Le but était d'attirer les clients grâce à un large éventail de produits de qualité, à la philosophie d'entreprise et à ses services.*

PAGES 106-107 ART DIRECTORS: *Steve Gibbs, Willie Baronet* DESIGNER: *Steve Gibbs* PHOTOGRAPHER: *Andy Post* ILLUSTRATOR: *Scott Donley* COPYWRITER: *Gail Hanna* AGENCY: *Gibbs Baronet* CLIENT: *Allsteel* COUNTRY: *USA* ■ *The directive in this project was to create brochures and sell sheets for all of the seating lines in the company's selection, instead of creating one large brochure. The challenge was to create a body of material with a common visual quality and voice while differentiating the features, functions, aesthetics and target market for each individual chair.* ● *Hier ging es nicht um eine umfangreiche Broschüre, sondern um einzelne Prospekte und Verkaufsblätter für alle Sitzmöbellinien der Firma. Die wichtigste Aufgabe war, einen einheitlichen Auftritt zu schaffen und gleichzeitig auf die individuellen Eigenschaften der einzelnen Stühle einzugehen.* ▲ *L'objectif de ce projet était de créer diverses brochures pour toutes les lignes de sièges et de chaises de la collection de la société, au lieu de créer une importante brochure. Le principal défi à relever était de créer une harmonie entre les différents supports publicitaires tout en faisant ressortir les caractéristiques de chaque chaise.*

PAGES 108-109 ART DIRECTORS: *Thomson Dawson, Bruce Kreps, George Gaskey* DESIGNER: *George Gaskey* PHOTOGRAPHERS: *William Sharpe, Dan Van Duinen, Effective Images* COPYWRITER: *Haworth, Inc.* AGENCY: *The Dawson & Company Creative Group* CLIENT: *Haworth, Inc.* COUNTRY: *USA* ■ *This brochure was designed to introduce a new product line geared to emerging work styles as well as to depict the client, a large manufacturer of office furniture, as an innovative and forward-thinking company.* ● *Bei dieser Broschüre ging es um die Einführung einer neuen Produktlinie für die sich abzeichnenden neuen Arbeitsgewohnheiten sowie um die Darstellung dieses Herstellers von Büromöbeln als eine innovative und zukunftsorientierte Firma.* ▲ *Cette brochure a été conçue pour lancer une nouvelle ligne de produits axée sur les styles de travail naissants. Elle présente également le client, un important fabricant de meubles de bureau, comme une société innovatrice et tournée vers le progrès.*

PAGE 110 ART DIRECTOR/ILLUSTRATOR/AGENCY: *Craig Frazier* COUNTRY: *USA* ■ *Self-promotional illustration brochure.* ● *Eigenwerbung eines Illustrators.* ▲ *Brochure autopromotionnelle d'un illustrateur.*

PAGE 111 ART DIRECTOR/ILLUSTRATOR/AGENCY: *João Machado* COUNTRY: *Portugal* ■ *This brochure showcases the illustrator's recent posters.* ● *In dieser Broschüre werden die neusten Plakate des Illustrators vorgestellt.* ▲ *Cette brochure montre les affiches récentes de l'illustrateur.*

PAGE 112 (TOP) ART DIRECTOR: *Robert Louey* DESIGNERS: *Robert Louey, Lisa Tauber* PHOTOGRAPHERS: *Various* ILLUSTRATOR: *Robert Louey* AGENCY: *Louey/Rubino Design Group* CLIENT: *Le Bar Bat* COUNTRY: *Hong Kong, United Kingdom*

PAGE 112 (CENTER) ART DIRECTOR: *Gene Seidman* DESIGNER: *Ana Rogers* AGENCY: *Rogers Seidman Design Team* CLIENT: *Campagna Restaurant* COUNTRY: *USA* ■ *The inspiration for this brochure stemmed from seeing Cinzano posters painted on the sides of barns dotting the Tuscan landscape. The design objective was to synthesize the essence of Tuscan cuisine with a New York edge.* ● *Inspiriert wurde diese Broschüre durch auf Wände gemalte Cinzano-Werbung in der Toskana. Das Ziel war, das Wesentliche der toskanischen Küche mit einem Touch vom New Yorker Lebensgefühl zu verbinden.* ▲ *Cette brochure s'inspire de publicités Cinzano peintes sur des façades en Toscanie. L'objectif était de faire transparaître l'essence de la cuisine toscane en y apportant une touche new-yorkaise.*

PAGE 112 (BOTTOM) ART DIRECTOR/DESIGNER/ILLUSTRATOR: *Robert Louey* AGENCY: *Louey/Rubino Design Group* CLIENT: *Zen Palate* ■ *This booklet and menu identity was created for an Asian, vegetarian restaurant in New York City.* ● *Speisekarte für ein vegetarisches asiatisches Restaurant in New York.* ▲ *Carte d'un restaurant asiatique de New York proposant des menus végétariens.*

PAGE 113 ART DIRECTOR: *Bob Dennard* DESIGNERS: *James Lacey, Chris Wood* PHOTOGRAPHER: *Brown Brothers Stock Photography* ILLUSTRATORS: *Various* COPYWRITERS: *Bob Dennard, Wayne Geyer* AGENCY: *Dennard Creative Inc.* CLIENT: *Bennigan's Restaurants* COUNTRY: *USA* ■ *This lunch menu was created for prototype test units throughout the United States.* ● *Dieses Mittags-Menu wurde von einer Restaurantkette in Testlokalen überall in den USA eingesetzt.* ▲ *Ce menu de déjeuners a été testé dans divers endroits d'une chaîne de restaurants aux Etats-Unis.*

PAGES 114-115 ART DIRECTOR: *Bridget de Socio* PHOTOGRAPHER: *Noel Allum* COPYWRITERS: *Jacqueline Yoakum, Eldon Wong* AGENCY: *Socio X* CLIENT: *Robert Schreiber* COUNTRY: *USA* ■ *Proposal for a centennial exhibition.* ● *Vorschlag für eine Hundertjahres-Ausstellung.* ▲ *Proposition pour une exposition centenaire.*

PAGES 116-117 DESIGNERS: *Karen Sisson, Kim Feasey* PHOTOGRAPHER: *David Hamilton* AGENCY: *DesignWorks* CLIENT: *Museum of New Zealand* COUNTRY: *New Zealand* ■ *This brochure promoted an exhibition that placed New Zealand art works in an historical context.* ● *Hier ging es um eine Ausstellung, in der Kunstwerke aus Neuseeland im Kontext mit historischen Ereignissen präsentiert werden.* ▲ *Cette brochure fait la promotion d'une exposition qui replaçait les travaux artistiques de la Nouvelle-Zélande dans un contexte historique.*

PAGES 118-119 ART DIRECTOR: *John Ball* DESIGNERS: *John Ball, Deborah Fukushima* AGENCY: *Mires Design, Inc.* CLIENT: *California Center for the Arts Museum* COUNTRY: *USA* ■ *Catalog for an exhibition of contemporary Californian sculpture. The artist's essays reflect their artwork, while the yellow stock paper keeps the essays visually separate from the coated artwork pages.* ● *Katalog für eine Ausstellung zeitgenössischer Skulpturen aus Kalifornien. Die Aufsätze des Künstlers sollten Spiegelbild seiner Skulpturen sein, wobei das gelbe Papier sie optisch von den Kunstdruckseiten mit den Abbildungen trennt.* ▲ *Catalogue pour une exposition de sculpture contemporaine californienne. Les essais de l'artiste reflètent son travail artistique, tandis que le papier jaune mat les différencie des pages d'illustrations sur papier brillant.*

PAGES 120-121 ART DIRECTOR/DESIGNER: *Stan Brod* PHOTOGRAPHER/COPYWRITER: *Corson Hirschfeld* AGENCY: *Wood/Brod Design* CLIENT: *Corson Hirschfeld, The Hennegan Company* COUNTRY: *USA* ■ *This publication was presented as a gift to friends and clients. The brochure showcases the geometric screening process and features photographs of ritual artifacts from museums and other collections in the US and Europe.* ● *Als Geschenk für Kunden und Freunde der Firma bestimmte Broschüre. Hier werden rituelle Gegenstände aus Museen und Sammlungen in den USA und Europa vorgestellt.* ▲ *Cette publication a été offerte en cadeau aux amis et aux clients. Elle présente les objets rituels et «mystérieux» en provenance de musées et de collections aux Etats-Unis et en Europe.*

PAGES 122-123 ART DIRECTOR: *John Ball* DESIGNERS: *John Ball, Gale Spitzley* COPYWRITER: *Reesey Shaw* AGENCY: *Mires Design* CLIENT: *California Center for the Arts Museum* COUNTRY: *USA* ■ *"Wildlife," the first exhibition at the California Center for the Arts Museum, looked at the animal world through the eyes of contemporary painters, sculptors, and photographers.* ● *Die erste Ausstellung des California Center of the Arts Museum war der künstlerischen Darstellung der Tierwelt durch zeitgenössische Maler, Bildhauer und Photographen gewidmet.* ▲ *«Faune et flore», la première exposition au California Center of the Arts Museum, présentait le monde des animaux à travers les yeux de peintres contemporains, de sculpteurs et de photographes.*

PAGE 124 ART DIRECTOR: *Paul Haslip* DESIGNER: *Dominic Ayre* PHOTOGRAPHERS: *Cylla Von Tiedemann, Beverly Rocket* COPYWRITER: *Paul Fraumeni* AGENCY: *HM+E Incorporated* CLIENT: *The National Ballet of Canada* COUNTRY: *Canada* ■ *This fbrochure was created for the capital campaign for the National Ballet of Canada's new facilities.* ● *Diese Broschüre diente als Instrument für eine Finanzierungskampage für die neuen Einrichtungen des kanadischen Nationalballetts.* ▲ *Cette brochure de souscription a été créée dans l'optique de collecter des fonds pour les nouvelles installations du Ballet National du Canada.*

PAGE 125 ART DIRECTOR/DESIGNER: *Sahin Aymerfen* PHOTOGRAPHER: *Stock* COPYWRITER: *Kayhan Yavuz* AGENCY: *Yorum-Publicis -FCB* CLIENT: *AB Sanat* COUNTRY: *Istanbul* ■ *This brochure was created for a ballet school.* ● *Broschüre für eine Ballett-Schule.* ▲ *Brochure d'une école de danse classique.*

PAGES 126-127 ART DIRECTOR: *Kenzo Izutani* DESIGNERS: *Kenzo Izutani, Aki Hirai* PHOTOGRAPHER: *Various* ILLUSTRATORS: *Goro Kiyosumi, George Ueki* AGENCY: *Kenzo Izutani Office Corporation* CLIENT: *A.Y.O Co., Ltd.* COUNTRY: *Japan* ■ *Pamphlet for Eikichi Yazawa's concert tour.* ■ *Prospekt für eine Konzert-Tournee.* ▲ *Brochure sur la tournée de concerts de Eikichi Yazawa.*

PAGES 128-129 ART DIRECTOR: *Don Sibley* DESIGNERS: *Don Sibley, Donna Aldridge* PHOTOGRAPHERS/ILLUSTRATORS: *Various* AGENCY: *Sibley/Peteet Design* CLIENT: *Weyerhaeuser Paper Company* COUNTRY: *USA* ■ *This brochure is part of a series entitled "American Artifacts" which takes a nostalgic look at America's legendary Route 66 highway.* ● *Die Broschüre gehört zu einer Serie mit dem Titel «Amerikanische Artefakten» und befasst sich mit der legendären Strasse durch die USA, der Route 66.* ▲ *Cette brochure fait partie d'une série intitulée «Œuvres américaines» et porte un regard nostalgique sur l'autoroute américaine 66, une légende.*

PAGES 130-131 ART DIRECTOR: *Kit Hinrichs* DESIGNERS: *Belle How, Amy Chan* PHOTOGRAPHER: *Gerald Bybee* ILLUSTRATOR: *Various* COPYWRITER: *Delphine Hirasuna* AGENCY: *Pentagram Design* CLIENT: *Simpson Paper Company* COUNTRY: *USA* ■ *This brochure from the "Tools of the Trade" series was created to promote brand recognition and product awareness for a recycled stock of paper.* ● *Die Broschüre gehört zu einer Reihe mit dem Titel «Werkzeuge der Branche» und informiert über die Eigenschaften von Recycling-Papieren.* ▲ *Cette brochure extraite d'une série a été réalisée pour promouvoir l'image de marque et les produits d'un fabricant de papier recyclé.*

PAGES 132-133 ART DIRECTOR: *Kit Hinrichs* DESIGNERS: *Belle How, Amy Chan* PHOTOGRAPHER: *Bob Esparza* ILLUSTRATOR: *Various* COPYWRITER: *Delphine Hirasuna* AGENCY: *Pentagram Design* CLIENT: *Simpson Paper Company* COUNTRY: *USA* ■ *Brochure from the "Tools of the Trade" series promoting the client's line of paper.* ● *«Werkzeuge der Branche» ist der Titel einer Serie von Broschüren, die über die Papiersorten von Simpson Paper informieren.* ▲ *Brochure de la série «Outils de la branche» destinée à la promotion des lignes de papier du client.*

PAGES 134-135 ART DIRECTOR: *Kit Hinrichs* DESIGNERS: *Belle How, Amy Chan* PHOTOGRAPHER: *Bob Esparza* ILLUSTRATOR: *Various* COPYWRITER: *Delphine Hirasuna* AGENCY: *Pentagram Design* CLIENT: *Simpson Paper Company* COUNTRY: *USA* ■ *This "Color on Color" brochure from the "Tools of the Trade" series demonstrates how colored papers can dramatically impact the look and feel of a printed piece when it is incorporated into the whole, rather than just the surface.* ● *Diese Broschüre mit dem Titel «Farbe auf Farbe» aus der Reihe «Werkzeuge der Branche» zeigt, wie wirksam farbiges Papier für Drucksachen eingesetzt werden kann.* ▲ *Cette brochure «Color on Color» de la série «Outils de la branche» montre l'impact que peuvent avoir des papiers couleur.*

PAGES 136-137 ART DIRECTOR: *Dana Arnett* DESIGNERS: *Curtis Schreiber, Fletcher Martin* PHOTOGRAPHER: *Scott Shigley* COPYWRITER: *John Nareski* AGENCY: *VSA Partners, Inc.* CLIENT: *Potlatch Corporation* COUNTRY: *USA* ■ *This Ben Day playbill was created for a paper company specializing in premium papers. It accompanies a promotional film which documents the fictional rise of the "world's greatest designer," Ben Day. The brochure provides humorous insight into the background of the fictional designer Ben Day while supporting the film's themes.* ● *Dieses Filmprogrammheft entstand im Auftrag eines Papierherstellers, der auf hochwertige Papierqualitäten spezialisiert ist. Es begleitet einen Werbefilm, der vom Aufstieg des «grossartigsten Designers der Welt», Ben Day, erzählt, einer fiktiven Figur. Mit viel Humor wird über des Leben Ben Days berichtet und auf die verschiedenen Themen des Films eingegangen.* ▲ *Ce programme a été réalisé pour un fabricant de papier de qualité. Il accompagne un film publicitaire consacré à Ben Day, le «meilleur designer au monde». Il présente avec beaucoup d'humour la vie de ce designer fictif et les thèmes du film.*

PAGES 138-139 ART DIRECTORS: *Rik Besser, Douglas Joseph* DESIGNER: *Rik Besser* PHOTOGRAPHER: *Terry Heffernan* COPYWRITER: *Margaret Burger* AGENCY: *Besser Joseph Partners* CLIENT: *Hopper Paper Company* COUNTRY: *USA*

PAGES 140-141 CREATIVE DIRECTORS: *Brad Copeland, George Hirthler* ART DIRECTOR/DESIGNER: *Raquel Corripio Miqueli* PHOTOGRAPHERS: *Various* SENIOR PRODUCTION ARTIST: *Donna Harris* COPYWRITERS: *Melissa James Kemmerly, Kim Dickinson* PRODUCTION MANAGER: *Laura Perlee* AGENCY: *Copeland Hirthler design + communications* CLIENT: *Neenah Paper* COUNTRY: *USA* ■ *"The Uncoated Truth" series was developed as a target multi-grade line paper promotion for specific end-use markets. The brochure targets the sports and recreation industries.* ● *Bei dieser Broschüre geht es um eine Kollektion unbehandelten Papiers in verschiedenen Stärken, das sich für spezielle Zwecke eignet. Die Sport-Broschüre richtet sich an die Sport- und Freizeitindustrie. Der Titel, «Die nackte (unbemäntelte) Wahrheit», ist ein Wortspiel mit dem englischen Ausdruck "uncoated".* ▲ *La série «La Vérité Dévoilée» a été développée en tant que promotion cible pour une gamme de papier de qualité destinée à des marchés spécifiques de consommateurs. La brochure sur les sports a été conçue pour l'industrie du sport et des loisirs.*

PAGE 142 ART DIRECTOR: *Paul Wharton* DESIGNER: *Tom Riddle* PHOTOGRAPHER: *Michael Crouser* ILLUSTRATOR: *David Plunkert* COPYWRITER: *Sandra Bucholz* AGENCY: *Little & Company* CLIENT: *Cross Pointe Paper Corporation* COUNTRY: *USA* ■ *"Passport to Cyberspace" positions the paper line as an appropriate paper choice for innovative design. It offers the graphic design audience information about the Internet and its resources, while demonstrating the paper's printability.* ● *Diese Broschüre über eine Papierqualität richtet sich an Graphiker und soll die Eignung des Papiers für innovatives Design demonstrieren. Sie enthält Informationen über das Internet und die verschiedenen Anbieter.* ▲ *Ce «Passeport pour le Cyberespace» présente une gamme de papier destinée au design d'innovation. Il fournit des renseignements sur le graphisme d'Internet et les ressources disponibles, tout en démontrant les possibilités d'impression du papier.*

PAGES 143 ART DIRECTOR: *Steve Pattee* DESIGNERS: *Steve Pattee, Kelly Stiles* PHOTOGRAPHER: *King Au* AGENCY: *Pattee Design, Inc.* CLIENT: *Fox River Paper* COUNTRY: *USA*

PAGES 144-145 CREATIVE DIRECTOR: *James A. Sebastian* ART DIRECTOR: *Margaret Biedel* DESIGNERS: *Margaret Biedel, Sarah Kloman* PHOTOGRAPHER: *Various* COPYWRITERS: *David Konigsberg, Brian Fingeret* AGENCY: *Designframe, Inc.* CLIENT: *Strathmore Papers* COUNTRY: *USA* ■ *"Solid Thinking" is a promotional brochure designed to introduce a paper line of six color choices.* ● *Gegenstand dieser Broschüre ist die Einführung einer Papierqualität, die in sechs Farben erhältlich ist.* ▲ *«Solid Thinking» est une brochure promotionnelle conçue dans le but de lancer une ligne de papier disponible dans six couleurs.*

PAGE 146 (LEFT) ART DIRECTOR/DESIGNER: *David Salanitro* PHOTOGRAPHER: *Sharon Beals* COPYWRITER: *Laura Smith* AGENCY: *Oh Boy, A Design Company* CLIENT: *Fox River Paper Company* COUNTRY: *USA* ■ *The client gave the word "dialect" around which to develop a concept and design for a brochure promoting a line of paper. This brochure, "The Dialect of Hip," was the result* ● *Das Motto für Konzept und Gestaltung dieser Broschüre über eine neue Papierqualität war «Dialekt», das Ergebnis: "The Dialect of Hip" (etwa «Die Sprache derjenigen, die voll durchsteigen»).* ▲ *Le client a imposé le mot «dialecte» pour développer le concept et le design d'une brochure faisant la publicité d'une ligne de papier. Cette brochure, «Le dialecte du Branché», en est le résultat.*

PAGE 146 (RIGHT) CREATIVE DIRECTORS: *Brad Copeland, George Hirthler* ART DIRECTOR/DESIGNER: *Raquel Corripio Miqueli* PHOTOGRAPHERS: *Various* COPYWRITER: *Melissa James Kemmerly* PRODUCTION MANAGER: *Laura Perlee* AGENCY: *Copeland Hirthler design + communication* CLIENT: *Neenah Paper* COUNTRY: *USA* ■ *The fashion brochure from "The Uncoated Truth" series was designed for the design and apparel industries. The concept was to demonstrate the greater quality and print versatility of uncoated papers to vertical markets which traditionally use slick coated paper for their print promotions.* ● *Hier geht ist um die Demonstration der verbesserten Druckqualität von Naturpapieren. Die Broschüre richtet sich an die Branchen, die normalerweise Hochglanzpapiere für die Print-Werbung einsetzen.* ▲ *Cette brochure de la série «La Vérité Dévoilée» a eté conçue pour les industries du* *design et de la mode. Il s'agissait de démontrer la qualité et les différentes possibilités d'impression des papiers bruts par rapport aux papiers brillants et lisses généralement utilisés en publicité dans ses secteurs.*

PAGE 147 Art Director: *Paul Wharton* Designer: *Tom Riddle* Photographer: *Geof Kern* Illustrator: *P. Scott Makela* Copywriter: *Laurel Harper* Agency: *Little & Company* Client: *Cross Pointe Paper Corporation* Country: *USA* ■ *"Times They Are A Changin" positions the client's paper as a choice for innovative design. It presents discussion about the changing technologies affecting graphic designers today, while demonstrating the paper's printability.* ● *Mit dieser Broschüre (mit dem Titel von Bob Dylan's berühmtem Song) wird Graphikern eine Papierqualität als Medium für innovatives Design angepriesen. Dabei werden die Fortschritte der neuen Technologie diskutiert, die grossen Einfluss auf die Arbeit der Graphiker haben.* ▲ *Cette brochure présente une qualité de papier destinée à des concepts de design novateurs. Elle contient des discussions sur les nouvelles technologies affectant les graphistes, tout en démontrant les possibilités d'impression du papier.*

PAGES 148-149 Art Directors: *Nick Ovendon, Andrew Cook* Designer: *Andrew Cook* Photographers/Illustrators: *Various* Copywriters: *Andrew Cook, David Lightman* Agency: *Design in Action* Client: *Arjo Wiggins Fine Papers* Countries: *United Kingdom and other European countries* ■ *This brochure was mailed to designers and printers throughout Europe.* ● *Diese Broschüre wurde an Graphiker und Drucker in ganz Europa verschickt.* ▲ *Cette brochure a été distribuée aux designers et imprimeurs à travers l'Europe.*

PAGES 150-151 Art Director: *Steve Liska* Designer: *Kim Fry* Photographer: *Steve Grubman* Agency: *Liska & Associates* Client: *Steve Grubman Photography* Country: *USA* ■ *This brochure showcases the photographer's specialty, animal photography.* ● *Hier geht es um das Spezialgebiet des Photographen, die Tierphotographie.* ▲ *Cette brochure montre la spécialité du photographe, la photographie animalière.*

PAGE 152 Designers: *Dennis Dimos, Tracy Mitsunaga* Photographer: *Vic Huber* Printer: *Woods Lithographics* Agency: *Mentus Inc.* Client: *Vic Huber Photography, Inc.* Country: *USA* ■ *This brochure introduces the photograper to design clients other than those that deal solely with the automotive industry.* ● *Eigenwerbung eines Photographen, der auch andere Bereiche ausser der Automobilphotographie beherrscht.* ▲ *Brochure autopromotionnelle d'un photographe qui maîtrise d'autres domaines que la photographie d'automobiles.*

PAGE 153 Art Director: *Brian Hawkins* Designer: *Janelle Aune* Photographer: *Brian Mark* Copywriter: *David Knudten* Agency: *Pierson Hawkins Inc. Advertising* Client: *Brian Mark Photography* Country: *USA* ■ *This brochure was created as a promotional piece for a photographer.* ● *Eigenwerbungsbroschüre eines Photographen.* ▲ *Brochure autopromotionnelle d'un photographe.*

PAGES 154-155 Art Directors: *Marcus Haslam, Tony Veazey* Designer: *Marcus Haslam* Photographer: *David Stewart* Copywriter: *Tony Veazey* Agency: *Broadbent, Cheetham, Veazey* Client: *David Stewart/Shed Films* Country: *Great Britain* ■ *This brochure of still photography accompanied the short film "Cabbage" directed by David Stewart for Shed Films.* ● *Diese Broschüre mit Stilleben begleitete den Kurzfilm "Cabbage" (Kohl), in dem David Stewart für Shed Films Regie führte.* ▲ *Cette brochure de photographies accompagne le court métrage «Cabbage» (Choux) mis en scène par David Stewart pour Shed Films.*

PAGE 156 Art Director: *Alexander Papesh* Designer: *Tim Ingersoll* Photographer: *Jay Koelzer* Copywriter: *Stewart Schley* Agency: *Lundwall Creative* Client: *Jay Koelzer Photography* Country: *USA* ■ *This self-promotional brochure announced a career move from newspapers to advertising. It was mailed to advertising agencies and select product companies in the US, Canada, and Japan.* ● *Mit dieser Broschüre sollten Werbeagenturen und bestimmte Hersteller in den USA, Kanada und Japan informiert werden, dass der ehemalige Zeitungsphotograph auf Werbephotographie umgestiegen ist.* ▲ *Cette brochure autopromotionnelle d'un photographe a annoncé un changement de carrière des journaux à la publicité. Elle a été distribuée aux agences de publicité et aux sociétés représentant des produits particuliers aux Etats-Unis, au Canada, et au Japon.*

PAGE 157 Designer: *Conrad Jorgensen Studio* Photographer: *Terry Heffernan* Prop Stylist: *Diane McGauley* Country: *USA* ■ *This promotional piece for print, film, and stock photography clients was a collaborative effort by the photographer, designer, and prop stylist.* ● *Diese Broschüre ist das Ergebnis einer Zusammenarbeit zwischen Gestalter, Photograph und Stylistin und wendet sich an potentielle Auftraggeber im Bereich der Print- und TV-Werbung sowie der Archiv-Photographie.* ▲ *Cette brochure est le fruit d'une collaboration entre photographe, designer et styliste. Elle s'adresse à des clients spécialisés dans la photographie d'archives, de films et d'imprimés.*

PAGES 158-159 Art Directors: *Ron Sullivan, Rob Wilson* Designer: *Rob Wilson* Photographer: *Fredrik Brodén* Copywriter: *Michael Langley* Agency: *Sullivan Perkins* Client: *Williamson Printing* Country: *USA* ■ *This brochure was created to demonstrate in-line coatings capabilities for a large, full-service printer.* ● *Mit dieser Broschüre wird das Können einer Full-Service-Druckerei im Bereich der Laminierung demonstriert* ▲ *Cette brochure présente le savoir-faire d'une imprimerie dans le domaine du couchage.*

PAGES 160-161 Agency: *Emery Vincent Design* Photographer: *Earl Carter* Copywriter: *David Webster* Client: *Spectro High Fidelity Colour Printers, Pty Ltd.* Country: *Australia* ■ *This brochure markets the services of a color printing company.* ● *Thema dieser Broschüre ist die von der Druckerei gebotene hohe Farbdruckqualität.* ▲ *Cette brochure commercialise les services d'une imprimerie spécialisée dans l'impression en couleur de haute fidélité.*

PAGE 162 Art Director: *Joerg Bauer* Photographers: *Joerg Bauer, Nils Schubert* Copywriter: *Peter Waibel* Agency: *Joerg Bauer Design* Client: *Filderandruck Studio* Country: *Germany*

PAGE 163 Art Directors: *Peter Good, Christopher Hyde* Designer: *Christopher Hyde* Photographers: *Peter Good, Christopher Hyde* Copywriter: *Christopher Hyde* Agency: *Cummings & Good* Client: *Chatham Printing Company, Inc.* Country: *USA* ■ *This brochure, created for a color sheet-fed commercial printer, showcases capabilities on a newly acquired six-color press.* ● *In dieser Broschüre geht es um die neu erworbene Sechs-Farben-Druckmaschine einer Druckerei.* ▲ *Cette brochure présente les possibilités d'une presse à six couleurs acquise récemment par une imprimerie.*

PAGES 164-165 Agency: *FHA Design* Copywriter: *Marjorie Johnston* Client: *Gunn and Taylor* Country: *Australia* ■ *Printer's promotion featuring the work of emerging Australian photographers.* ● *In dieser Broschüre für eine Druckerei werden die Arbeiten von jungen australischen Photographen vorgestellt.* ▲ *Promotion de l'imprimeur présentant le travail de jeunes photographes australiens.*

PAGES 166-167 Art Director/Designer: *Achim Jäger* Photographer: *Thomas Hahn* Illustrator: *Udo Benz* Copywriter: *Peter Waibel* Agency: *Jäger & Waibel Werbeagentur GmbH* Client: *Haller Druck GmbH* Country: *Germany* ■ *This brochure informs clients and potential customers about the printer's move into a larger office space.* ● *Diese Broschüre informiert über den Ausbau der Druckerei und den Umzug in ein neues, grösseres Gebäude.* ▲ *Cette brochure informe les clients actuels et potentiels de l'expansion des bureaux de l'imprimeur et de l'emménagement dans un complexe plus grand.*

PAGES 168-171 Art Directors/Designers: *Philippe Saglio, Philippe Wolff* Editor: *Philippe Saglio* Client: *Laguiole* Country: *France* ■ *This brochure for Laguiole, a pocket knife with slightly curved handle and elongated blade, focuses on the success story of its manufacturers in central France. In keeping up with the times, they had called Philippe Starck and other designers to enlarge upon the company's classic range of knifes.* ● *Das berühmte 'Laguiole', gemäss Larousse «ein Taschenmesser mit leicht gekrümmtem Griff und verlängerter Klinge» sowie die Erfolgsgeschichte seiner Hersteller in Frankreich sind das Thema dieser Broschüre. Um zeitgemäss zu bleiben, hatte die Firma vor Jahren Philippe Starck und andere Designer um eine Erweiterung der klassischen Produktlinie gebeten.* ▲ *Le célèbre couteau Laguiole ainsi que l'histoire de son fabricant sont au centre de cette brochure. La société a demandé à divers designers tels que Philippe Starck de donner un look plus moderne au produit.*

PAGES 172-173 Art Directors: *Allison Muench, JP Williams* Photographer: *William Abranowicz (Art + Commerce)* Copywriter: *Laura Silverman* Agency: *design: M/W* Client: *Takashimaya New York* Country: *USA* ■ *This is the fourth catalog in a series promoting the store's gift merchandise.* ● *Der vierte aus einer Reihe von Katalogen für die Geschenkartikel des Ladens in New York.* ▲ *Quatrième catalogue d'une série sur les articels cadeau du magasin.*

PAGES 174-175 Art Director: *Massimo Vignelli* Designers: *Massimo Vignelli, Dani Piderman* Photographers: *Luca Vignelli (portrait), J.P. Luthy (watch)* Client: *Pierre Junod Watches* Country: *Switzerland* ■ *This brochure publicizes a new watch, "Halo," designed by Lella and Massimo Vignelli, with interchangeable colored bezels.* ● *Hier wird die neue Uhr «Halo» vorgestellt. Sie wurde von Lella und Massimo Vignelli aus New York entworfen und hat austauschbare, farbige Fassungen.* ▲ *Cette brochure présente la nouvelle montre «Halo» conçue par Lella et Massimo Vignelli.*

PAGES 176-177 Art Directors: *Charles S. Anderson, Todd Piper-Hauswirth* Designer: *Todd Piper-Hauswirth* Photographers: *Darrell Eager, Paul Irmiter* Illustrator: *CSA Archive* Copywriter: *Lisa Pemrick* Client: *CSA Archive* Country: *USA* ■ *This is a catalog of CSA Archive products based on original and historic line art images.* ● *Dieser Katalog informiert über das Produktangebot des CSA-Archivs, das auf historischen Vorlagen basiert.* ▲ *Catalogue des produits CSA Archive fondé sur des images artistiques originales et historiques.*

PAGES 178-179 Art Director/Designer: *Steve Sandstrom* Photographer: *Sjef Wildschut* Copywriter: *Steve Sandoz* Agency: *Artsy-Fartsy Productions* Agency: *Sandstrom Design* Client: *Soloflex, Inc.* Country: *USA* ■ *This brochure was used as a response to inquiries generated by television and print advertising for personal home weight training machines sold through direct advertising and mail order.* ● *Diese Broschüre informiert über im Direktverkauf angebotene Fitness-Geräte für private Haushalte, für die beim Publikum der Fernseh- und Printmedienwerbung Informationsbedarf bestand.* ▲ *Cette brochure donne des informations sur des appareils de fitness destinés aux ménages.*

PAGES 180-181 Art Director: *Jack Anderson* Designers: *Jack Anderson, David Bates* Photographer: *Darrell Peterson* Illustrator: *Todd Connor* Copywriter: *Julie Huffaker* Agency: *Hornall Anderson Design Works, Inc.* Client: *SunDog, Inc.* Country: *USA* ■ *This catalog serves as an image and advertising piece for the company's travel packs, accessories, and soft goods. The copy was written in a travel journal format, using 'destination' copy for the different product categories.* ● *Image- und Werbebroschüre einer Firma, die Reiseausstattungen anbietet. Die Texte lesen sich wie die eines Reisejournals, wobei den einzelnen Produktkategorien bestimmte Reiseziele zugeordnet sind.* ▲ *Brochure publicitaire destinée à promouvoir l'image de marque d'une société spécialisée dans les articles de voyage. La répartition des gammes de produits est faite en fonction des destinations.*

PAGES 182-183 Art Director/Designer: *Scott Mires* Photographer: *Chris Wimpey* Handlettering: *Judythe Sieck* Agency: *Mires Design, Inc.* Client: *Taylor Guitars* Country: *USA* ■ *This brochure showcases a limited edition acoustic guitar series.* ● *In diesem Katalog wird eine limitierte Edition einer akustischen Gitarre vorgestellt.* ▲ *Cette brochure présente une série limitée de guitares acoustiques.*

PAGE 184 ART DIRECTOR: *Randall Hull* DESIGNER: *Karen Kwan* PHOTOGRAPHER: *John Huet* COPYWRITER: *Timothy Cohrs* AGENCY: *Patrick Mountain Advertising* CLIENT: *Lai Venuti Lai Advertising* COUNTRY: *USA* ■ *This brochure is part of a repositioning campaign for an ad agency in the Silicon Valley. The concept took form in ads, new ID and this promotional leave-behind.* ● *Die Broschüre ist Teil einer Kampagne, mit der sich eine Werbeagentur im Silicon Valley neu positionieren will. Zum Konzept gehören ausserdem Anzeigen und ein neues Erscheinungsbild.* ▲ *Cette brochure fait partie d'une campagne de repositionnement d'une agence de publicité dans la Silicon Valley. Le concept englobe des annonces-presse, une nouvelle identité, et cette brochure.*

PAGE 185 ART DIRECTOR/DESIGNER: *Tim Bruce* DESIGN DIRECTOR: *Ted Stoik* AGENCY: *VSA Partners, Inc.* PHOTOGRAPHER: *Stock* CLIENT: *Jack Macholl* COUNTRY: *USA*

PAGE 186 ART DIRECTORS: *Paul F. Schifino, J. Kenneth Wright* DESIGNER: *Paul F. Schifino* AGENCY: *Vance Wright Adams & Associates, Inc.* CLIENT: *Bayer USA* COUNTRY: *USA* ■ *For this brochure, the client wanted a promotional piece that would grab attention.* ● *Promotion für den Chemie- und Pharmakonzern Bayer in den USA, der etwas besonders Auffälliges gewünscht hatte.* ▲ *Pour cette brochure, le client voulait quelque chose de frappant.*

PAGE 187 ART DIRECTOR/DESIGNER: *Kathleen Phelps* PHOTOGRAPHER: *Various* COPYWRITER: *Camille Cozzone* AGENCY: *Platinum Design Inc., NYC* CLIENT: *Times Mirror* COUNTRY: *USA* ■ *This media kit was created to market both FIELD & STREAM and OUTDOOR LIFE. The client requested a high profile piece which would both celebrate the 100th anniversary of FIELD & STREAM as well as introduce a new multimedia organization. Since the main purpose of the media kit was to sell ad space in the magazines, it had to reflect the full-color, outdoor photography inherent in both magazines without looking too upscale.* ● *Dieser Media-Kit für die Zeitschriften FIELD & STREAM und OUTDOOR LIFE wurde anlässlich des 100jährigen Bestehens von FIELD & STREAM und zur Einführung einer neuen Multimedia-Organisation erstellt. Da der Hauptzweck der Inseratenverkauf in den Zeitschriften war, ging es um die Präsentation der für beide Magazine typischen farbigen Landschaftsaufnahmen, ohne teuer zu wirken.* ▲ *Ce «kit» média a été créé dans le but de commercialiser à la fois FIELD & STREAM et OUTDOOR LIFE. Le client a exigé un produit qui célèbre non seulement le centenaire de FIELD & STREAM, mais qui introduit également une nouvelle organisation multimédia. Comme le but principal du «kit» média était de vendre des espaces publicitaires dans des magazines, il devait présenter des photographies de paysages en couleurs typiques pour les deux magazines, sans paraître trop haut de gamme.*

PAGES 188-189 ART DIRECTOR/DESIGNER: *Russell Fong* PHOTOGRAPHER: *John Clang* ILLUSTRATOR: *Jumali Katani* COPYWRITERS: *Ian Batey, Tim Evill* AGENCY/CLIENT: *Batey Ads Singapore* COUNTRY: *Singapore* ■ *This brochure portrays the agency's Asian heritage to potential clients.* ● *Hier werden asiatische Motive verwendet, um die asiatische Tradition der Werbeagentur hervorzuheben.* ▲ *Cette brochure utilise des graphiques asiatiques pour mettre en valeur l'héritage asiatique de l'agence.*

PAGES 190-191 ART DIRECTOR: *Reiner Hebe* DESIGNERS: *Anda Manea, Britta Moarefi, Joachim Reyle* PHOTOGRAPHER: *Various* ILLUSTRATOR: *Mike Loos* COPYWRITER: *Reiner Hebe* AGENCY/CLIENT: *HEBE Werbung & Design* COUNTRY: *Germany* ■ *This brochure was created for self promotion.* ● *Eigenwerbung einer Werbe- und Design-Agentur.* ▲ *Publicité autopromotionnelle d'une agence de publicité et de design.*

PAGES 192-193 ART DIRECTORS: *Paul Curtin, Keith Anderson* DESIGNER: *Keith Andersen* PHOTOGRAPHERS: *Barry Robinson, Keith Sylva, Julian Zogoda* COPYWRITER: *Eric Osterhaus* AGENCY: *Goodby Silverstein & Partners* CLIENT: *Bell Helmets* COUNTRY: *USA* ■ *Bell Sports products mass market catalog.* ● *Ein Katalog für Bell-Sportartikel, die für Grossverteiler bestimmt sind.* ▲ *Catalogue des articles de sport Bell.*

PAGE 194 ART DIRECTOR/DESIGNER: *Ron Dumas* PHOTOGRAPHER: *Gary Hush* COPYWRITER: *Bob Lambie* AGENCY/CLIENT: *Nike, Inc.* COUNTRY: *USA* ■ *This brochure was created for the launch of a new corporate identity program for Nike.* ● *Thema dieser Broschüre ist die Lancierung eines neuen Erscheinungsbildes von Nike.* ▲ *Cette brochure a été créée pour lancer un nouveau programme sur l'identité de l'entreprise Nike.*

PAGE 195 ART DIRECTOR: *Michael Tiedy* DESIGNER: *Grey Matter, Benton Wong* PHOTOGRAPHER: *Gary Hush* AGENCY: *Nike, Inc.* CLIENT: *Nike, Inc.* COUNTRY: *USA* ■ *Inflatables brochure.* ● *Broschüre für aufblasbare Produkte.* ▲ *Brochure des produits gonflables.*

PAGES 196-197 ART DIRECTOR/DESIGNER: *Dan Richards* COPYWRITER: *Stanley Hainsworth* AGENCY/CLIENT: *Nike, Inc.* COUNTRY: *USA* ■ *This brochure was designed to teach consumers about the four Nike F.I.T.* ● *Mit dieser Broschüre sollen die Konsumenten über die Eigenschaften der vier F.I.T.-Stoffe von Nike informiert werden.* ▲ *Cette brochure a été conçue pour informer les consommateurs sur les quatre textiles Nike F.I.T.*

PAGES 198-199 CREATIVE DIRECTOR: *Michael Jager* ART DIRECTOR: *David Covell* DESIGNERS: *Jim Anfuso, David Covell, Ken Eiken, John Phemister, Dan Sharp, Mark Sylvester* PHOTOGRAPHER: *Geoff Fosbrook* ILLUSTRATOR: *Jim Anfuso, John Churchman* PROJECT COORDINATOR: *David Schriber* AGENCY: *Jager Di Paola Kemp Design* CLIENT: *Burton Snowboards* COUNTRY: *USA* ■ *For this brochure, the design company wanted to present the snowboard company as a technology leader. To do so, "sonic" colors, techno diagrams, a custom font, and a robot tour guide were used.* ● *Hier wird ein Snowboard-Hersteller als technologisch führend präsentiert. Verschiedene optische Elemente im Katalog unterstreichen diesen Anspruch.* ▲ *Pour cette brochure, la société de design désirait présenter le fabricant de snowboards comme un leader en technologie. Divers éléments visuels du catalogue soulignent cet aspect.*

PAGES 200-201 ART DIRECTOR: *Ruth Tulino* DESIGNER: *Walter Herrington* PHOTOGRAPHER: *Peter Hogg* ILLUSTRATOR: *Laurie Gerns* COPYWRITER: *Bernadette Soter* AGENCY: *Tulino Design, Inc.* CLIENT: *B. Via International Housewares, Inc.* COUNTRY: *USA* ■ *The brochure was designed as part of the product launch for Via International Housewares and provides a buying guide for key retailers.* ● *Diese Broschüre ist Teil einer Produkteinführung und dient dem Einzelhandel als Bestellkatalog.* ▲ *Cette brochure conçue pour Via International Housewares fournit un guide d'achat pour les principaux détaillants.*

PAGE 202 (LEFT) ART DIRECTOR/DESIGNER: *Mark Krumel* ILLUSTRATOR: *Michael Linley Illustration* COPYWRITER: *Paula Jurcenko* AGENCY: *Rickabaugh Graphics* CLIENT: *Huntington Banks* COUNTRY: *USA* ■ *This brochure for a bank with an investment division complements a verbal and computer presentation.* ● *Diese Broschüre dient einer Bank als ergänzendes Informationsmittel über ihre Investment-Abteilung, deren Dienstleistungen auch im persönlichen Gespräch und per Computer demonstriert werden.* ▲ *Brochure pour une banque avec un département spécialisé dans les placements. Elle coïncide avec une présentation verbale et sur ordinateur.*

PAGE 202 (RIGHT) ART DIRECTOR/DESIGNER: *João Machado* PHOTOGRAPHER: *Luis Ferreira Alves* ASSISTANT COORDINATOR: *Joana Leão* CLIENT: *Ippar* COUNTRY: *Portugal* ■ *This brochure was published for the renewal of St. John's Theatre in Portugal.* ● *Zur Wiedereröffnung des St. John's-Theater in Porto herausgegebene Broschüre.* ▲ *Cette brochure a été publiée pour la rénovation du Théâtre St. John's au Portugal.*

PAGE 203 ART DIRECTOR: *Michael Denny* DESIGNERS: *John Bateson, Jonathan Simpson, Rachael Dinnis, Tim Flach* PHOTOGRAPHER: *Damien Gillie* AGENCY: *Roundel Design Group* CLIENT: *Czech Technology Park* COUNTRY: *Germany, France, Japan, England, Czech Republic* ■ *This brochure was created as part of a corporate identity and promotional campaign with international appeal.* ● *Mit dieser Promotionsbroschüre für einen Technologiepark in Tschechien soll ein internationales Publikum angesprochen werden.* ▲ *Brochure créée pour développer une identité institutionnelle et une campagne promotionnelle destinée à un public international.*

PAGE 204-205 ART DIRECTOR/DESIGNER: *Randall Hill* PHOTOGRAPHER: *Richard Myers Photography* COPYWRITER: *Rosewood Hotels & Resorts* AGENCY: *David Carter Design Associates* CLIENT: *P.T. Binapuri Lestari* COUNTRY: *Indonesia* ■ *This brochure was developed to create local interest in a new spa and club being developed in Jakarta, Indonesia.* ● *Mit dieser Broschüre soll das Interesse der lokalen Bevölkerung an einem neuen Sport- und Fitness-Club in Jakarta geweckt werden.* ▲ *Cette brochure devait susciter l'intérêt de la population locale pour un nouveau club de sport et de remise en forme à Djakarta.*

PAGE 206-207 ART DIRECTORS: *Scott Timms, Phillip Smith* DESIGNER: *Pam Stone* AGENCY: *Nordenson Lynn Advertising* CALLIGRAPHER: *Rob Waters* ILLUSTRATOR: *Bob Conge* COPYWRITER: *Mike Nevin* CLIENT: *Rain Bird* COUNTRY: *USA* ■ *This brochure for a leading manufacturer of irrigation products was part of a multifaceted campaign developed for the company's commercial division and was intended to re-establish the company's products as the predominate offering in the category.* ● *Diese Broschüre für einen Hersteller von Bewässerungsprodukten gehört zu einer umfassenden Kampagne der Firma, mit der ihre führende Stellung im Markt gefestigt und das umfassende Produktangebot präsentiert werden soll.* ▲ *Conçue pour un fabricant de produits d'arrosage et d'irrigation, cette brochure s'insère dans une vaste campagne qui devait consolider la position de leader du fabricant sur le marché et présenter son importante gamme de produits.*

PAGE 208 ART DIRECTORS: *Paul Black, Thomas Vasquez* DESIGNER/ILLUSTRATOR: *Staci Fisher* COPYWRITER: *Jack Wooley* DESIGN FIRM: *Squires & Company* CLIENT: *Los Rios Anglers* COUNTRY: *USA* ■ *This brochure is an easy-to-use reference guide on how to tie knots while fly-fishing. The two-color design was produced economically and at a size that would fit in a fly fisherman's vest.* ● *Ein zweifarbig gedrucktes Instruktionsbüchlein für das Binden von Knoten beim Fliegenfischen, das klein genug ist, um in die Westentasche des Anglers zu passen.* ▲ *Petit manuel imprimé en deux couleurs sur la manière de nouer des nœuds lors de la pêche à la mouche. Grâce à son format, il se glisse aisément dans une poche de gilet.*

....
DESIGN FIRMS · AGENCIES
....

PHOTOGRAPHERS · ILLUSTRATORS · COPYWRITERS

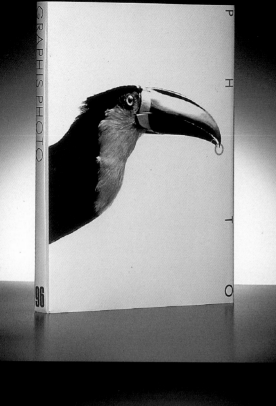

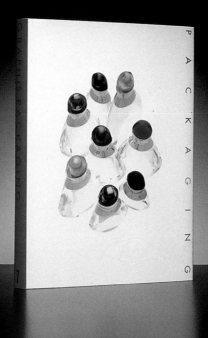

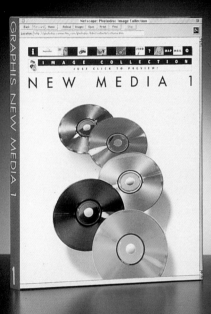

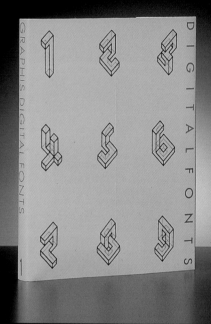

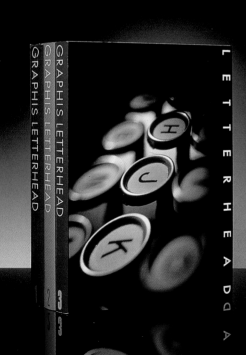

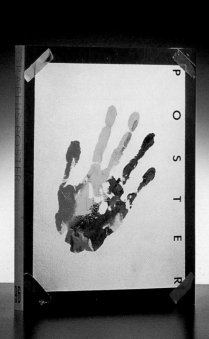

G R A P H I S   B O O K S

BOOKS		ALL REGIONS
☐ BLACK & WHITE BLUES (HARDCOVER)	US$	69.95
☐ BLACK & WHITE BLUES (PAPERBACK)	US$	45.95
☐ GRAPHIS ADVERTISING 97	US$	69.95
☐ GRAPHIS ALTERNATIVE PHOTOGRAPHY 95	US$	69.95
☐ GRAPHIS ANNUAL REPORTS 5	US$	69.95
☐ GRAPHIS BOOK DESIGN	US$	75.95
☐ GRAPHIS BROCHURES 2	US$	75.00
☐ GRAPHIS CORPORATE IDENTITY 2	US$	75.95
☐ GRAPHIS DESIGN 97	US$	69.95
☐ GRAPHIS EPHEMERA	US$	75.95
☐ GRAPHIS FINE ART PHOTOGRAPHY	US$	85.00
☐ GRAPHIS INFORMATION ARCHITECTS	US$	49.95
☐ GRAPHIS MUSIC CDS	US$	75.95
☐ GRAPHIS NUDES (PAPERBACK)	US$	39.95
☐ GRAPHIS PACKAGING 7	US$	75.00
☐ GRAPHIS PHOTO 96	US$	69.95
☐ GRAPHIS POSTER 96	US$	69.95
☐ GRAPHIS PRODUCTS BY DESIGN	US$	69.95
☐ GRAPHIS SHOPPING BAGS	US$	69.95
☐ GRAPHIS TYPOGRAPHY 1	US$	69.95
☐ GRAPHIS TYPE SPECIMENS	US$	49.95
☐ **GRAPHIS PAPER SPECIFIER SYSTEM (GPS)**	US$	495.00
** ADD $30 SHIPPING/HANDLING FOR GPS		
☐ HUMAN CONDITION	US$	49.95
☐ SHORELINE	US$	85.95
☐ WATERDANCE (PAPERBACK)	US$	24.95
☐ WORLD TRADE MARKS 1OO YRS.(2 VOL. SET)	US$	250.00

NOTE! NY RESIDENTS ADD 8.25% SALES TAX

☐ CHECK ENCLOSED (PAYABLE TO GRAPHIS)
    (US$ ONLY, DRAWN ON A BANK IN THE USA)

USE CREDIT CARDS (DEBITED IN US DOLLARS)

☐ AMERICAN EXPRESS   ☐ MASTERCARD   ☐ VISA

CARD NO.   EXP. DATE

CARDHOLDER NAME

SIGNATURE

(PLEASE PRINT)

NAME

TITLE

COMPANY

ADDRESS

CITY

STATE/PROVINCE   ZIP CODE

COUNTRY

SEND ORDER FORM AND MAKE CHECK PAYABLE TO:
GRAPHIS INC.,
141 LEXINGTON AVENUE, NEW YORK, NY 10016-8193, USA

G R A P H I S   M A G A Z I N E

MAGAZINE	USA	CANADA	SOUTHAMERICA/ ASIA/PACIFIC
☐ ONE YEAR (6 ISSUES)	US$ 89.00	US$ 99.00	US$ 125.00
☐ TWO YEARS (12 ISSUES)	US$ 159.00	US$ 179.00	US$ 235.00
☐ AIRMAIL SURCHARGE (6 ISSUES)	US$ 59.00	US$ 59.00	US$ 59.00

☐ ONE YEAR (6 ISSUES)   US$ 59.00
    FOR STUDENTS WITH COPY OF VALID STUDENT ID AND
    PAYMENT WITH ORDER

☐ CHECK ENCLOSED   ☐ PLEASE BILL ME

USE CREDIT CARDS (DEBITED IN US DOLLARS)

☐ AMERICAN EXPRESS

☐ MASTERCARD

☐ VISA

CARD NO.   EXP. DATE

CARDHOLDER NAME

SIGNATURE

(PLEASE PRINT)

NAME

TITLE

COMPANY

ADDRESS

CITY

STATE/PROVINCE   ZIP CODE

COUNTRY

SERVICE BEGINS WITH ISSUE THAT IS CURRENT WHEN
ORDER IS PROCESSED.

SEND ORDER FORM AND MAKE CHECK PAYABLE TO:
GRAPHIS INC.,
141 LEXINGTON AVENUE, NEW YORK, NY 10016-8193, USA

(C9B0A)